4

INSIDE WRITING

The Academic Word List in Context

Nigel A. Caplan

Jennifer Bixby

SERIES DIRECTOR:

Cheryl Boyd Zimmerman

OXFORD
UNIVERSITY PRESS

OXFORD
UNIVERSITY PRESS

198 Madison Avenue
New York, NY 10016 USA

Great Clarendon Street, Oxford, OX2 6DP, United Kingdom

Oxford University Press is a department of the University of Oxford.
It furthers the University's objective of excellence in research, scholarship,
and education by publishing worldwide. Oxford is a registered trade
mark of Oxford University Press in the UK and in certain other countries

Director, ELT New York: Laura Pearson
Head of Adult, ELT New York: Stephanie Karras
Senior Development Editor: Wiley Gaby
Executive Art and Design Manager: Maj-Britt Hagsted
Design Project Manager: Michael Steinhofer
Content Production Manager: Julie Armstrong
Production Artist: Julie Sussman-Perez
Image Manager: Trisha Masterson
Production Coordinator: Christopher Espejo

ISBN: 978 0 19 460146 7 STUDENT BOOK

Printed in China

This book is printed on paper from certified and well-managed sources

ACKNOWLEDGEMENTS

*The authors and publisher are grateful to those who have given permission to reproduce
the following extracts and adaptations of copyright material:*

pp. 62–63 From "An Introduction to Multitasking and Texting: Prevalence
and Impact on Grades and GPA in Marketing Classes" by Dennis E. Clayson
and Debra A. Haley, *Journal of Marketing Education,* April 2013, Vol. 35, No. 1,
pp. 26–40. Copyright by SAGE Publications. Reprinted by Permission of SAGE
Publications.

p. 78 From questions on pp. 18–19, 21, and 84–85 from *The Economic Naturalist:
Why Economics Explains Almost Everything* by Robert H. Frank, copyright © 2007.
Reprinted by permission of Basic Books, a member of the Perseus Books
Group and The Random House Group Limited.

p. 79 From "Why are hotel prices in Sharm El Sheikh in Egypt lowest during
periods of highest occupancy?" by Rhoda Hadi from *The Economic Naturalist:
Why Economics Explains Almost Everything* by Robert H. Frank, copyright © 2007.
Reprinted by permission of Basic Books, a member of the Perseus Books
Group and The Random House Group Limited.

p. 80 From "Why are child safety seats required in cars but not in airplanes?"
by Greg Balet from *The Economic Naturalist: Why Economics Explains Almost
Everything* by Robert H. Frank, copyright © 2007. Reprinted by permission of
Basic Books, a member of the Perseus Books Group and The Random House
Group Limited.

p. 157 From "What Humans Know that Watson Doesn't" by Trevor Pinch
from CNN.com, February 28, 2011 © 2011 Cable News Network, Inc. All rights
reserved. Used by permission and protected by the Copyright Laws of the
United States. The printing, copying, redistribution, or retransmission of this
Content without express written permission is prohibited.

p. 158 From "Did the Olmec Know How to Write?" by Karen O. Bruhns and
Nancy L. Kelker, Science, March 9, 2007, Vol. 315, No. 5817, pp. 1365–1366.
Reprinted by permission of Karen Olsen Bruhns and Nancy L. Kelker.

p. 158 From "Claim of Oldest New World Writing Excites Archaeologists"
by Andrew Lawler, Science (News), September 15, 2006, Vol. 313, No. 5793,
p. 1551. Reprinted by permission of the author.

Illustrations by: 5W Infographics, pgs. 64, 78, and 142.

*We would also like to thank the following for permission to reproduce the following
photographs:* **Cover**, Doug Landreth/Corbis; Jerry Hoare/Illustration Works/
Corbis; Gary Buss / Getty Images; Peter Beavis / Getty Images; Photocuisine
/ Masterfile; catwalker / shutterstock; Jennifer Gottschalk/shutterstock;
Alloy Photography / Veer. **Interior**, p1 Michael Shay/Shutterstock; p2 Blend
Images LLC/Corbis UK Ltd; p15 www.thepaintingfool.com/The Painting Fool;
p17 www.thepaintingfool.com/The Painting Fool; p31 Michael Shay/Getty
Images; p32 Bill Peters/The Denver Post via Getty Images/Getty Images; p34
Ivan Vdovin/Jai/Corbis UK Ltd; p47 Gallo Gusztav/Alamy; p48 imagebroker/
Alamy; p61 Alina Vincent Photography, LLC/Getty Images; p77 Jens Lucking/
Shutterstock; p79 John Warburton-Lee/Getty Images; p80 2007 China Photos/
Shutterstock; p93 Ingvar Bjork/Fotolia; p94 Jan Scherders/Oxford University
Press; p109 Maxim_Kazmin/Fotolia; p110 funkyfood London - Paul Williams/
Alamy; p112 Sam Bloomberg-Rissman/Getty Images; p125 tony french/Alamy;
p126 Yang Shichao/Xinhua Press/Cor/Corbis UK Ltd; p127 Javier Larrea / age
fotostock/Superstock Ltd.; p128 Javier Larrea / age fotostock/Superstock Ltd.;
p141 National Geographic Image Collection/Alamy; p143 World Pictures /
Alamy (Mayan statue); p143 age fotostock/Superstock Ltd. (Olmec statue); p157
Associated Press/Press Association Images.

Acknowledgements

We would like to acknowledge the following individuals for their input during the development of the series:

Salam Affouneh
Higher Colleges of Technology
Abu Dhabi, U.A.E.

Kristin Bouton
Intensive English Institute
Illinois, U.S.A.

Nicole H. Carrasquel
Center for Multilingual Multicultural Studies
Florida, U.S.A.

Elaine Cockerham
Higher College of Technology
Muscat, Oman

Danielle Dilkes
CultureWorks English as a Second Language Inc.
Ontario, Canada

Susan Donaldson
Tacoma Community College
Washington, U.S.A

Penelope Doyle
Higher Colleges of Technology
Dubai, U.A.E.

Edward Roland Gray
Yonsei University
Seoul, South Korea

Melanie Golbert
Higher Colleges of Technology
Abu Dhabi, U.A.E.

Elise Harbin
Alabama Language Institute
Alabama, U.S.A.

Bill Hodges
University of Guelph
Ontario, Canada

David Daniel Howard
National Chiayi University
Chiayi

Leander Hughes
Saitama Daigaku
Saitama, Japan

James Ishler
Higher Colleges of Technology
Fujairah, U.A.E.

John Iveson
Sheridan College
Ontario, Canada

Alan Lanes
Higher Colleges of Technology
Dubai, U.A.E.

Corinne Marshall
Fanshawe College
Ontario, Canada

Christine Matta
College of DuPage
Illinois, U.S.A.

Beth Montag
University at Kearney
Nebraska, U.S.A.

Kevin Mueller
Tokyo International University
Saitama, Japan

Tracy Anne Munteanu
Higher Colleges of Technology
Fujairah, U.A.E.

Eileen O'Brien
Khalifa University of Science, Technology, and Research
Sharjah, U.A.E.

Jangyo Parsons
Kookmin University
Seoul, South Korea

John P. Racine
Dokkyo Daigaku
Soka City, Japan

Scott Rousseau
American University of Sharjah
Sharjah, U.A.E.

Jane Ryther
American River College
California, U.S.A

Kate Tindle
Zayed University
Dubai, U.A.E.

Melody Traylor
Higher Colleges of Technology
Fujairah, U.A.E.

John Vogels
Higher Colleges of Technology
Dubai, U.A.E.

Kelly Wharton
Fanshawe College
Ontario, Canada

Contents

The Inside Track to Academic Success

Student Books

For additional student resources visit: www.oup.com/elt/insidewriting

iTools for all levels

The *Inside Writing* iTools is for use with an LCD projector or interactive whiteboard.

Resources for whole-class presentation
> **Book-on-screen** focuses class on teaching points and facilitates classroom management.
> **Writing worksheets** provide additional practice with the genre and Writing Models.

Resources for assessment and preparation
> Customizable Unit, Mid-term, and Final Tests evaluate student progress.
> Answer Keys and Teaching Notes

Additional instructor resources at: www.oup.com/elt/teacher/insidewriting

UNIT

1

Energy Drinks

In this unit, you will

> analyze how arguments are used in academic essays.
> use arguments and counterarguments.
> increase your understanding of the target academic words for this unit.

WRITING SKILLS

> Supporting an Argument
> Counterarguments
> **GRAMMAR** Subject-Verb Agreement

Self-Assessment

Think about how well you know each target word, and check (✓) the appropriate column. I have…

TARGET WORDS	never seen this word before.	heard or seen the word but am not sure what it means.	heard or seen the word and understand what it means.	used the word confidently in *either* speaking or writing.
AWL				
amend				
🔑 behalf				
constitute				
🔑 core				
discriminate				
🔑 federal				
implicit				
🔑 inevitable				
legislate				
🔑 ministry				
🔑 panel				
🔑 pursue				
🔑 sufficient				
suspend				

🔑 Oxford 3000™ keywords

Building Knowledge

Read these questions. Discuss your answers in a small group.

1. Do you drink caffeinated beverages such as coffee, tea, or soda? How does caffeine affect you?

2. Do you think that energy drinks, which are flavored drinks that contain caffeine, are safe for young children or teenagers? Why, or why not?

3. Are there any restrictions on the sale of energy drinks in your area? Explain.

Writing Model

An argument essay is a typical academic assignment in which the writer presents a point of view and then supports it. Read a student's argument essay about the regulation of energy drinks.

No Regulation on Energy Drinks

Energy drinks, which have been growing in popularity around the world in recent years, are now attracting the attention of politicians in the United States. That is not a good sign. Some **legislators** want to ban[1]
5 the sale of these drinks to minors (children 18 and under). This is because energy drinks have recently become very popular with teenagers. Because they contain caffeine, some health experts are worried about the effects on adolescents' minds and bodies. However,
10 there are strong reasons why we should not ban the sale of energy drinks to minors.

Most young people drink coffee regularly.

First, it is important to understand how caffeine affects the body. Caffeine is a widely available natural ingredient and has been consumed by billions of people around the world for centuries.
15 It is found in coffee, tea, and soda, and even in some nonprescription medications. Caffeine stimulates the central nervous system. It works by blocking natural sedatives[2] from nerve receptors[3] in the brain. As a result, it increases energy and makes a person feel more awake.

Many people believe that energy drinks contain extremely high amounts of caffeine,
20 making them **implicitly** dangerous for children and teenagers. In fact, energy drinks do not contain excessive[4] amounts of caffeine. Popular energy drinks can have from 80 to 138 milligrams of caffeine in 8 ounces. Compare that to an 8-ounce cup of coffee which has 165 milligrams of caffeine. Most energy drinks have less caffeine than a cup of coffee from your

---

[1] *ban:* decide officially that something is not allowed
[2] *sedatives:* substances that make someone go to sleep or make the person feel calm and relaxed
[3] *nerve receptors:* nerve endings in the body that react to changes and make the body react in a particular way
[4] *excessive:* greater than what seems reasonable or appropriate

neighborhood coffee shop. No one seems concerned about teens buying coffee. Therefore,
25 why should the government ban energy drinks when they contain less caffeine than a
strong cup of coffee?

Recently a **panel** of health experts called for a nationwide **suspension** of sales of
energy drinks to minors. This reflects the general belief that too much caffeine is
dangerous for children. However, there is **insufficient** evidence to support these fears. In
30 the scientific community, questions continue as to exactly how much of a health risk
energy drinks are. In contrast, there is scientific evidence that caffeine has some
important health benefits. For instance, it can help people who don't get enough sleep to
stay awake. It can improve physical performance, relieve headaches, and help certain
medical conditions. There is no clear evidence of the harmful effects of caffeine on
35 children or teenagers, only fears.

Some people feel that the **federal** government should follow the example of other
countries. Countries such as Denmark and Turkey have banned energy drinks, but that
fact alone should not guide actions in the United States. The **federal** government should
not rely on the health **ministries** in other countries for new **legislation**. The U.S. Food
40 and Drug Administration (FDA) is in charge of ensuring the safety of foods and drinks. It
approved the ingredients in energy drinks years ago. The FDA concluded that none of the
ingredients in energy drinks is harmful when consumed in reasonable quantities. Energy
drinks have been available in the United States for decades without **constituting** a
significant public health problem. Therefore, there is no reason why the **federal**
45 government should **amend** its decision now.

History has shown that bans on consumer products usually fail. For example, bans on
the sale of cigarettes to minors have not kept teenagers from smoking. Banning the sale
of energy drinks to minors would **inevitably** make the drinks even more appealing to
young people. If the government wants to protect the health of teenagers, surely it cannot
50 think that banning energy drinks will keep them out of young hands. The better
approach is through education. Teenagers need to learn that almost any product
consumed in excess can be dangerous, from water to sugar to caffeine. They need to
learn to **discriminate** between good and poor nutritional choices. Individuals, including
teenagers, need to be responsible for their own decisions.

55 At the **core** of this energy drink ban is the issue of who is responsible for the health
of children—the government or parents. Clearly parents should make the decisions about
what their children should eat and drink, whether their children are 6 or 16. Parents
should guide their children's decisions and help them learn to consume without
overconsuming. The **federal** government must trust that parents will make the right
60 choices for their children's health. Citizens do not want politicians to **legislate** how to
raise children.

Unless scientists prove that caffeine is harmful to minors, politicians should not
pursue a ban on the sale of energy drinks. Energy drinks, soda, and coffee have all been
available to all ages for many years. These drinks have not caused health problems for the
65 average person. The FDA has already approved the ingredients of energy drinks.
Furthermore, a ban would limit our individual choices. The **federal** government should
not make drink choices on our **behalf**. Rather, parents should educate their children to
consume energy drinks responsibly.

LEARN

When you write about a point of view, give an opinion, or support a plan of action, you use arguments to support your ideas and to persuade the reader. There are four major types of persuasion, called appeals. They are:

1. logical appeals using facts, evidence, and common knowledge;

2. emotional appeals trying to trigger feelings or touch upon personal values;

3. appeals using the authority and reliability of the writer and the writer's sources; and

4. appeals emphasizing the urgency of a situation.

You can combine more than one appeal to support your arguments, or you can use them separately. Make your decision based on your audience and the purpose of your writing. What will readers find most persuasive—an emotional argument, a personal argument, or an argument supported by logic and facts?

APPLY

A. Read arguments based on the writing model. Write the type of appeal for each one. You will use one type of appeal twice.

appeal to emotions	common knowledge
appeal to logical thinking	facts or statistics

1. The government should not limit our personal drink choices.

   appeal to emotions

2. Energy drinks have recently become very popular with teenagers.

   _____

3. An 8-ounce cup of coffee has about 165 milligrams of caffeine.

   _____

4. Coffee contains caffeine, but we don't restrict its sale to teenagers. Why should we ban energy drinks, which also contain caffeine?

   _____

5. The U.S. FDA approved energy drinks years ago, and there have not been significant health problems. So, why should the FDA ban energy drinks now?

   _____

B. Look at the argument essay on pages 2–3 again. Choose the best answer for each statement.

1. The writer has chosen to use mostly ____ in the arguments.

   a. facts and statistics

   b. appeals to logical thinking and facts

   c. emotional appeals

2. The writer could strengthen the arguments by ____.

   a. adding more factual information

   b. using the first person (*I*) to show personal opinion

   c. including information about the writer's background and reliability

3. The writer did not include an appeal about the urgency of the situation because ____.

   a. people have been drinking coffee for centuries

   b. there are no urgent or specific deadlines for the legislation

   c. changes in legislation take a long time

Analyze

A. Reread the writing model on pages 2–3. Number the statements to show the order of the arguments.

____ 1. Most energy drinks have less caffeine than a cup of coffee from your neighborhood coffee shop.

____ 2. Banning the sale of energy drinks to minors will not stop young people from obtaining and drinking them. It is more effective to educate teens.

____ 3. Parents, not the government, should decide what their children are allowed to drink.

____ 4. Caffeine is a natural ingredient that stimulates the central nervous system.

____ 5. Instead of a ban on the sale of energy drinks, parents should educate their children about responsible consumption.

____ 6. The FDA approved energy drink ingredients as safe years ago, so it should not amend its decision without scientific proof that the drinks are harmful.

____ 7. There is no clear evidence that energy drinks are harmful to children, but there is evidence that caffeine can provide some health benefits.

____ 8. Although some legislators want to ban the sale of energy drinks to minors, this is not a good idea.

B. With a partner, compare your answers to activity A. Then discuss these questions.

1. Overall, does the essay start with facts and statistics or with appeals to logical thinking?

2. Why does the writer use this order of arguments and appeals?

C. Answer the following questions.

1. What is the purpose of the first paragraph?

   a. to explain what the issue is

   b. to state the issue and give the writer's general opinion

   c. to preview for the reader what arguments the writer will make

2. What is the purpose of the second paragraph?

   a. to give background information to the reader

   b. to summarize common knowledge (what everyone already knows)

   c. to show that many common drinks contain caffeine

3. What are the main points that the writer makes in the conclusion? Circle one, two, or three answers.

   a. There is insufficient evidence of the health risks of caffeine.

   b. The government should not make choices for us.

   c. Parents should educate their children about energy drinks.

D. Discuss these questions in a small group.

1. Look at the five arguments presented in the body paragraphs of the essay. Which argument do you think is the strongest one? Why?

2. Which argument do you think is the weakest one? Why?

3. What is your personal opinion about the topic? Do you agree or disagree with the writer? Explain your answer.

Vocabulary Activities   STEP I: Word Level

The prefix *in-* can be added to some adjectives to make them negative.

Sufficient means "enough for a particular purpose." *Insufficient* means "not large, strong, or important enough."

   Allow yourself **sufficient** time to get to the airport.

   His salary is **insufficient** for living in the city.

Other adjectives with this prefix include *inaccessible*, *inactive*, *inaccurate*, *incapable*, *incomplete*, and *insignificant*.

Note that not all words starting with *in-* have commonly-used opposite adjectives. *Inevitable*, meaning "unavoidable," is a common term. The adjective *evitable* is very rarely used.

CORPUS

A. Complete the paragraph with adjectives from the box. You will use one word twice.

inactive	inevitable	insufficient	sufficient

High school students often neglect their health. For example, they typically do not get (1) ___sufficient___ sleep due to their busy schedules. Most students are often (2) ___inactive___, spending much of their time seated while studying and attending class. In addition, many students skip breakfast in the morning, not realizing that (3) ___insufficient___ nutrition will make it hard for them to concentrate in class. Although stress is a(n) (4) ___inevitable___ part of student life, there are ways to manage it. School administrators should emphasize the study of nutrition and health to ensure students receive (5) ___sufficient___ preparation for living a healthy life.

Legislate means "to make a law." It has many word forms that are related to government. For instance, there are three noun forms.

Legislation is a law or set of laws passed by a government body.

A **legislator** is a member of a group of people who have the power to make laws.

A **legislature** is a group of people who have the power to make and change laws.

CORPUS

B. Complete the sentences with the correct form of the word *legislate*.

1. Three politicians are running in the election. Only one will become a ___legis___.

2. The students spent many hours discussing the new _____ about public health clinics.

3. Some people believe that the government should not _____ the use of nutritional supplements.

4. The student government has officers and a _____ of 20 students.

Word Form Chart		
Noun	**Verb**	**Adjective**
amendment	amend	_____
constitution	constitute	constitutional
discrimination	discriminate	discriminatory
federation	_____	federal

C. Complete the sentences using target words from the word form chart. Change the noun or verb form as needed.

1. Australia began as a _____ when six British colonies joined together to start a new country.

2. After it wrote a _____ to govern the country, it became the Commonwealth of Australia in 1901.

3. A _federal_ government makes decisions that affect an entire nation.

4. After a new law is proposed, legislators debate it and make _____ to the law.

5. It is unusual for a judge to _____ a decision that was made in a trial. Usually there are no changes.

6. In most countries, it is illegal to _discriminate_ against a person based on his or her race.

7. In the past, there were a number of _amendment_ laws, but these have been eliminated.

Vocabulary Activities   STEP II: Sentence Level

The noun *core* can mean "the center part of a piece of fruit or an object." It can also mean "the most important part of something, such as an idea or argument."

> *The **core** of the apartment is the kitchen.*

> *He has made the environment the **core** of his economic policy.*

The adjective *core* means "most important; main or essential."

> *Her **core** values were shaped by growing up in a religious household.*

CORPUS

D. Answer the questions with complete sentences. Use the word *core*. Then compare your answers with a partner.

1. Which parts of the apple do you avoid eating?

2. Do you think that health should be a core subject in school?

3. Describe a core belief that you have about nutrition.

4. Who is in your core group of friends?

E. Match the target word with the words it can collocate with. Write the letter.

<u>C</u> 1. have ＿＿＿＿＿＿ faith, trust, or belief in

<u>D</u> 2. a prime, senior, or health ＿＿＿＿＿＿

<u>E</u> 3. solar, control, or wood ＿＿＿＿＿＿

<u>A</u> 4. ＿＿＿＿＿＿ a dream, goal, or career

<u>B</u> 5. ＿＿＿＿＿＿ payment, production, a license, or a search

a. pursue

b. suspend

c. minister

d. implicit

e. panel

F. Write a sentence with each of the target words (*implicit, minister, panel, pursue,* and *suspend*) in activity E. Use collocations.

1. I have implicit trust in her honesty.

2. The minister will arrive on Monday.

3. The university is hosting a panel on free speech.

4. I wants to pursue a career in medicine.

5. We can suspend the rules just this one.

To do something *on someone's behalf* means you do something "for someone as his or her representative or instead of him or her."

   *I asked the question <u>on her **behalf**</u>.*

The phrase can also mean "because of someone or for someone."

   *I felt very upset <u>on his **behalf**</u>.*

 CORPUS

G. Complete the sentences in your own words. Use *behalf* and the correct possessive form.

1. The younger brother is very shy, so ＿＿＿＿＿＿＿＿＿.

2. I asked my professor to write ＿＿＿＿＿＿＿＿＿.

3. Since the prime minister cannot attend the meeting, ＿＿＿＿＿＿＿＿＿.

4. Some employees experienced discrimination on the job, so a lawyer filed a

   complaint ＿＿＿＿＿＿＿＿＿.

Grammar | Subject-Verb Agreement

Most cases of subject-verb agreement are simple, such as remembering to add an -s to the verb in the third person (*she writes, he shows*). However, in some situations, subject-verb agreement is more complex.

1. Indefinite pronouns (*someone, anything, nobody, everyone*) are always singular.

   Everyone agrees that parents should monitor what their children consume.

2. In formal writing, none is singular.

   None of the ingredients in energy drinks **is** harmful.

3. The main noun of a phrase may be separated from the verb.

   One of the new drinks **is** especially popular with teenagers.

4. The verb in an adjective clause must agree with its subject.

   Legislators who **want** to ban energy drinks have written a new bill.

5. Clauses and gerunds are singular.

   What researchers discovered was that there are other stimulating ingredients in energy drinks.

6. Irregular plural forms are plural (*people, children, men, women, data*).

   People are confused about the ingredients.

A. Underline the subject for each verb in parentheses and circle the correct verb form.

1. For <u>children</u> who ((participate)/ participates) in sports, water is the best drink.

2. People (think / thinks) that sports drinks, which are also very popular with children, (is / are) a good alternative to water.

3. What distinguishes sports drinks from energy drinks (is / are) that sports drinks do not contain caffeine.

4. Sports drinks are intended to help athletes who (has / have) exercised vigorously replace liquids that (was / were) lost through sweating.

5. Consuming sports drinks (is / are) not recommended because they typically (contain / contains) large numbers of calories.

B. Read the sentences. Correct the errors in subject-verb agreement.

1. Doctors should educate parents and children about the health risks of energy and sports drinks and explains the difference between the types of drinks.

2. Sports drink ads aimed at young people tends to mislead.

3. The labeling on sports drinks fail to properly inform the public.

4. Children who is involved in sports should drink water rather than sports drinks that contains many calories.

5. Most children thinks that sports drinks will improve their performance.

WRITING SKILL   Counterarguments

LEARN

When writing an argument essay, your point of view will be stronger if you include the counterarguments. Counterarguments are the other side of your viewpoint. They show that you have considered other points of view.

Introduce the counterargument using one of these phrases:

It is true that … ; Supporters/opponents claim that … ; Some might argue that … ; Many people believe that … ; It might be said that …

Use a transition and then state your refutation. This will explain why the opposite point is invalid.

Nevertheless; However; On the other hand; In fact; While that is true,

> **It is true** that caffeine may overstimulate a person's nervous system. **However**, it is not the government's job to control how much caffeine a person drinks.

APPLY

A. Reread the essay on pages 2–3 and find two counterarguments. Underline the introduction to the counterargument and the transition to the argument.

B. For each statement below, write a counterargument to introduce it based on the ideas in the essay on pages 2–3. You may revise the beginning of the statements.

1. *Opponents to a ban claim that the FDA has already approved the ingredients in energy drinks. While that is true, it is not the whole story. In fact, the*

   The FDA has classified energy drinks as dietary supplements, so there are not the same limits on the amount of caffeine in an energy drink as in soda, which is classified as a beverage. The FDA is basically avoiding the issue of regulating these drinks. They should be regulated as beverages.

2. _____

   _____

   Health officials in the United States only started recording health problems with energy drinks in 2010. In Germany, where they have followed this issue since 2002, many serious health problems have been recorded.

3. _____

   _____

   Many energy drink labels do not list the amount of caffeine in a serving because companies are not required to do so. Some of the larger serving sizes of energy drinks contain up to 240 milligrams of caffeine.

Collaborative Writing

A. With a partner, fill in the chart with ideas for a paragraph supporting a ban on the sale of energy drinks to minors. Select an argument made in the writing model and give your counterargument.

Introduction: Explain the situation and state your position on the issue.	
Explanation: Briefly explain why it is an important health issue.	
Counterargument	
Argument and support	
Conclusion	

B. With your partner, write your argument paragraph. Include a counterargument.

C. With another pair of students, compare your paragraphs. Answer these questions.

1. Where is the argument stated? Is the position on the issue clear?

2. Is there a brief explanation of the issue? How are your explanations different?

3. What other support is used? What kind of appeal are you using to persuade the reader? (See page 4.)

Independent Writing

A. To prepare to write an argument essay, read the topic questions below and give your point of view in a brief answer to each question.

1. Should high schools in your area ban the sale of soda and sugary drinks to students?_____

2. Should universities require students to take a physical education or health class?_____

B. Read the student notes below. Check the information that you may be able to use in an essay about sodas and sugary drinks in high schools.

> Should schools control what students buy? What about parents?
> Students are told junk food is bad, but it is sold at school.
> Soda vending machines are a major source of income for schools.
> Educate children, but let them make their own choices.
> Do sodas and sugary drinks cause obesity (overweight children)?
> If banned, students will just buy sugary drinks elsewhere.
> Centers for Disease Control 2011 study: Water and milk are the most popular teen beverages, followed by fruit juice and soda.
> A can of soda contains 18 teaspoons of sugar and 240 calories.

C. Select a topic for your argument from activity A or your own idea related to health. Consider both sides of the argument. Make a list of points in the T-chart. Then check (✓) the strongest argument.

Topic:	
For:	**Against:**

D. Discuss your ideas in a small group. Talk about what persuasive points you will make and how you can support your arguments with appeals.

E. Fill in the chart with notes to plan your essay. Use at least one counterargument.

Introduction: Explain the situation and what the proposal is. State your thesis, that is, your position on the issue.	
Explanation: Give background information. Why is it important?	
Is there a counterargument? Provide argument and support.	
Is there a counterargument? Provide argument and support.	
Is there a counterargument? Provide argument and support.	
Conclusion:	

F. Review your arguments and support by considering these questions.

1. For each argument, think about persuading your reader. Are you using logical reasoning, appealing to emotions or shared values, or using facts and statistics?

2. Which argument is the strongest? Where will you place it in your essay? Why?

3. Do you need any additional information to strengthen your arguments?

G. Write your argument essay. Use your planning notes. Include at least one counterargument. Use target vocabulary from the unit.

A. Read your argument essay. Answer the questions below, and make revisions as needed.

1. Check (✓) the information you included in your argument.

☐ clear statement of your thesis or point of view

☐ background information

☐ at least one counterargument

☐ explanation of the issue

☐ arguments that include appeals

☐ a conclusion

2. Look at the information you did not include. Would adding that information make your argument stronger?

Grammar for Editing | Checking Verbs

1. Most arguments are written in the present simple tense because they describe facts, opinions, or general truths.

2. Examples from specific times in the past should be written in past simple tense.

3. Statements about ongoing events, recent changes, or research summaries should be written in the present perfect (for example, *ministers have become concerned; the energy drinks market has grown; researchers have studied the effects of caffeine*).

Check for the correct verb tenses as you edit your writing.

B. Check the language in your essay. Revise and edit as needed.

Language Checklist
☐ I used target words in my argument essay.
☐ I included counterarguments and supported my arguments with appeals.
☐ I used correct subject-verb agreement.
☐ I used the correct verb tenses.

C. Check your essay again. Repeat activities A and B.

Self-Assessment Review: Go back to page 1 and reassess your knowledge of the target vocabulary. How has your understanding of the words changed? What words do you feel most comfortable using now?

UNIT 2

Can Computers Be Creative?

In this unit, you will

> analyze a summary and response and learn how it is used in academic writing.
> use summary, interpretation, and evaluation.
> increase your understanding of the target academic words for this unit.

WRITING SKILLS

> Summary
> Paraphrasing
> **GRAMMAR** Reduced Adjective Clauses

Self-Assessment

Think about how well you know each target word, and check (✓) the appropriate column. I have...

TARGET WORDS	never seen this word before.	heard or seen the word but am not sure what it means.	heard or seen the word and understand what it means.	used the word confidently in *either* speaking or writing.
AWL				
analogy				
bias				
🔑 capacity				
🔑 commission				
🔑 derive				
infer				
interpret				
manipulate				
🔑 notion				
notwithstanding				
🔑 pose				
🔑 prospect				
radical				
sphere				

🔑 Oxford 3000™ keywords

Building Knowledge

Read these questions. Discuss your answers in a small group.

1. What kinds of art do you enjoy?

2. Do you think computers can create original artwork?

3. What do you think is the difference between intelligence and creativity?

Writing Model

A summary and response is a class assignment in which you summarize the main ideas of an article and give your opinion about it. Read an online article about a computer that makes art and a student's summary of the article and response to it.

THE CODE TO CREATIVITY

BY ANDREW AIRE

Artists' studios are places of creativity: half-finished **commissions**, spilled paint, bright sunlight streaming through large windows. However, one controversial British artist works in a very different space, a dimly lit computer laboratory at Goldsmiths College, London. That's because The Painting Fool is
5 a computer program. Its creator, though, is certainly human. He is Dr. Simon Colton, a professor of computer science and a leading expert in the field of computational creativity. Colton has caused quite a stir in the painting world with his software. What is that stir all about? Colton's work has raised questions about whether a computer can produce imaginative works of art. If
10 software, and not just its designer, can be said to be creative—then what does it mean to be human? Can something that does not have feelings generate art that produces feelings in us?

I traveled to London to investigate these questions. At first, I was highly doubtful about the **prospect** of feeling emotions looking at computer-
15 generated art. Now, I am not so sure. But let me first explain what The Painting Fool is not. It is not software used by a human artist to create images and graphics. It is not a program for **manipulating** photographs. And it is not a robot that applies paint to a canvas under the direction of a real person. Those are all tools supporting human creativity, but the machines
20 themselves are not creative.

Colton's goal with The Painting Fool was far more **radical**. He wanted "to build a software system that is one day taken seriously as a creative artist in its own right."[1] At first, it could only take existing photographs and apply different styles and techniques to produce an original piece. Some of these early works are quite pleasing, but they are **derivative**, hardly the output of a creative artist. The second stage in the software's development was to add human emotion. So Colton and two colleagues gave The Painting Fool the **capacity** to **infer** emotions from a photograph. To test it, they took still images from a popular French movie. The resulting series of 220 paintings, called *Amelie's Progress*, is quite remarkable. In each one, the computer chose a different combination of colors, style, and media.[2] Amazingly, the software was able to depict the feelings of the main character at each moment. Looking at the painting, I was almost persuaded that The Painting Fool was painting with emotion like any "real" artist.

However, Colton's claim goes further: He argues on his website that The Painting Fool is imaginative. This is a complex **notion**. It implies that a computer can generate its own subjects and create art that does not already exist in reality. Surely a program that can only **manipulate** *0*s and *1*s can only produce abstract[3] designs using mathematical formulas. But no. One painting for a 2011 exhibition consists of dozens of small landscapes, each one slightly different. Colton calls it *Four Seasons* (the computer's creativity apparently does not extend to writing titles!). The trees and clouds are not drawn from photographs. Instead, the software has **derived** realistic images from its knowledge of nature and art. The result is a wholly original but not very exciting canvas.

Landscapes from *Four Seasons*, created by The Painting Fool

I'm not convinced that *Four Seasons* is a masterpiece.[4] I agree with *New Scientist* reviewer Catherine de Lange that the effect is rather "mechanical." Colton would respond that I am being unfair to The Painting Fool. He'd say that if my young son had done this painting without looking at a photograph, I would have called his work imaginative. Yes, I would, and then I would have called the newspapers. Seriously, though, from that perspective, it is hard to deny that Colton has a point. The Painting Fool is not a great artist, but it is creative. And now it's branching out[5] into sculpture, animation, and poetry. Somehow, though, I'm not worried for my job. At least, not yet.

---

[1] *in its own right:* because of its qualifications or efforts
[2] *media:* the materials or the forms that an artist, a writer, or a musician uses
[3] *abstract:* not representing people or things in a realistic way, but rather expressing the artist's ideas about them
[4] *masterpiece:* a work of art that is an excellent example of art in general
[5] *branch out:* to start to do an activity that has not been done before

Julie Lang
ART 102
September 23

The Code to Creativity: Summary and Response

Andrew Aire **poses** a **radical** question in his recent article: Do computers have the **capacity** to be creative? He introduces Simon Colton, a computer scientist from Goldsmiths College, London. Colton designed software called The Painting Fool. The program does not actually paint, but it creates digital art based on photographs, other art,
5 and knowledge of the world. Aire agrees with an art critic, Catherine de Lange, that the results are "mechanical." However, he also admits to having a **bias** against computer-generated art. Colton defends his software by making an **analogy** with a child's painting, convincing the author. Like a child, the computer is learning to use its imagination to be creative.

10 However, I disagree with Aire's **interpretation** that The Painting Fool displays creativity. **Notwithstanding** rare cases, computers can never truly **pose** as humans. This is especially true in the artistic **sphere**. Good art is a product of emotion. It is a creative act, expressing the artist's view of the world. A computer cannot have these thoughts, so the output of The Painting Fool will never have any depth. Paintings generated by
15 software cannot be meaningful because computers can only **manipulate** ideas, patterns, and images that already exist. They cannot make anything truly original or think like humans.

Colton's argument is that his software can learn to be creative just like a child. However, I think there is an important difference between a child and a computer.
20 Children's paintings represent their developmental stage. Their art changes over time because their technical skill improves and also because they have experiences that influence their paintings and drawings. The computer is influenced only by the code[1] that runs it and the websites it searches. It may be able to find patterns in people's faces, but it cannot **infer** human emotions from photographs. In short, The Painting Fool is
25 not learning, and it is certainly not producing art.

---

[1] *code:* a system of computer-programming instructions

LEARN

A summary is a common academic assignment, often as part of a longer paper. A good summary includes the main ideas from the original text, is organized logically, and is written in your own sentences. To summarize an article:

1. Read the article several times. Make sure you understand it thoroughly.

2. Identify the author's main idea, focus, or argument. Rewrite this main idea using your own words.

3. Divide the article into sections. Use subheadings and transition words to help you.

4. For each section of the article, identify and label its main idea or purpose. If the article doesn't have subheadings, add your own.

5. Organize the section labels you identified in step 4 logically.

6. Write your summary, starting with the main idea of the whole article. Then fill in the details for each section.

7. Check your sentences to make sure that they are not too similar to the ones in the original article.

APPLY

A. Which of these subheadings could you add to Andrew Aire's article on pages 16–17?

- ☑ 1. Who Is Simon Colton?
- ☐ 2. History of Computerized Art
- ☐ 3. What Is The Painting Fool?
- ☐ 4. Other Creative Computers
- ☐ 5. The Development of The Painting Fool
- ☐ 6. Is The Painting Fool Creative?

B. With a partner, discuss why you chose the subheadings you did in activity A. Which paragraph(s) would you label with your selected subheadings?

C. Which paragraphs from the original article do these sentences summarize? Write the correct paragraph number.

_1_ 1. Andrew Aire poses a radical question in his recent online article: Do computers have the capacity to be creative?

____ 2. He introduces Simon Colton, a computer scientist from Goldsmiths College.

____ 3. The program does not actually put paint on paper, but it creates digital art based on photographs, other art, and knowledge about the world.

____ 4. Although Aire agrees with another reviewer that one recent painting is "mechanical," he admits that he The Painting Fool is creative.

____ 5. Colton defends his software by making an analogy with a child's painting, which the author finds convincing.

Analyze

A. Read the student's summary and response again on page 18. Does each paragraph of the student's assignment contain information from the article, the student's opinion, or both? Check the correct boxes.

Paragraph	Summary: Information from the article	Response: Student's opinion
1		
2		
3		

B. Does the student agree or disagree with these ideas from the article? What reasons does the student give?

1. The Painting Fool is creative.

   Agree / Disagree. Why? _____

2. The analogy of a child learning to draw demonstrates that The Painting Fool produces imaginative art.

   Agree / Disagree. Why? _____

3. The computer can infer emotions from pictures.

   Agree / Disagree. Why? _____

C. Are the following statements from the response a summary (S), an opinion (O), or a reason (R)?

_S_ 1. The program does not actually paint, but it creates digital art based on photographs, other art, and knowledge of the world.

___ 2. However, I disagree with Aire's interpretation that The Painting Fool displays creativity.

___ 3. Good art is a product of emotion.

___ 4. Colton's argument is that his software can learn to be creative just like a child.

___ 5. However, I think there is an important difference between a child and a computer.

___ 6. Children's paintings represent their developmental stage.

D. Discuss these questions in a small group.

1. Do you think the student wrote a good summary of the article? Why, or why not?

2. Do you agree with the student's response to the article?

3. What would you write in response to this article?

Vocabulary Activities STEP I: Word Level

Word Form Chart		
Noun	**Verb**	**Adjective**
interpretation	interpret	interpretive
interpreter	misinterpret	
manipulation	manipulate	manipulative
prospect	_____	prospective

A. Complete the paragraph using words from the word form chart.

Computer software has been developed that can grade students' writing. However, the computer cannot really (1) _____interpret_____ essays. Instead, it has lists of words and phrases that it expects to find in essays on each topic. This makes some professors worried that (2) _____ students could potentially (3) _____ the system and earn higher scores than they deserve. This (4) _____ has led the test designers to install systems to protect against such (5) _____.

Imply and *infer* have related meanings. When writers, speakers, and artists *imply* something, they express or suggest something without stating it directly. When readers, listeners, and viewers *infer* something from the text or artwork, they reach an opinion or conclusion about it.

I did not mean to **imply** any criticism of your book.

We can **infer** the artist's intentions by viewing a few of his paintings.

The related nouns are *implication* and *inference*.

CORPUS

B. Complete the sentences with the correct form of *imply* or *infer*.

1. The _____ of this research is that robots can replace humans for certain tasks.

2. Computers can find basic information in texts but can't make _____.

3. It can be _____ from the graph that the cost of producing robots will probably decrease dramatically in the next ten years.

4. What are you _____ about my painting? Don't you like it?

C. Complete the lists with words from the box that have similar meanings. You will not use one of the words.

bias	notion	pose	radical
capacity	notwithstanding	prospect	sphere

1. ball / globe / _____sphere_____

2. idea / concept / _____

3. however / on the other hand / _____

4. ability / competence / _____

5. extreme / revolutionary / _____

6. prejudice / one-sided / _____

Vocabulary Activities   STEP II: Sentence Level

D. Complete the sentences with the correct form of the target vocabulary in the box to create a common collocation with the underlined words.

commission	derive	pose	public	radically

1. The Painting Fool has recently entered the _____public_____ <u>sphere</u> with its tour of exhibitions and press releases.

2. The Painting Fool is _____ <u>different</u> from other image-manipulation software.

3. Its inventor _____ <u>a question</u>: Can a computer be creative?

4. Would you want to _____ <u>a painting</u> from a computer?

5. An artist _____ <u>enjoyment from</u> the creative process. If a computer can't feel, how can it recreate feelings in its art?

E. Write new sentences with the collocations you created in activity D from the target vocabulary and the underlined words.

1. *Artists often wait to display their best work in the public sphere.* _____

2. _____

3. _____

4. _____

5. _____

An *analogy* is a comparison made between two things in order to explain a complex idea.

> Cooking is a common **analogy** for the writing process.

Verbs that collocate with analogy include *draw, suggest,* and *extend.* To *stretch* an analogy means "to take an analogy too far so that it may no longer be useful."

> The reviewer <u>draws an **analogy** between</u> painting and dreaming.

> It's <u>stretching an **analogy**</u> to say that computers are like children learning to paint.

The adjective form is *analogous* (meaning "similar or comparable").

> The results are **analogous to** those obtained in earlier studies.

CORPUS

F. Are the following good analogies? Write sentences using the different forms of the words *analogy* or *analogous* in parentheses.

1. A reliable person is like a rock. (analogous to) *This is a good analogy because rocks are strong and don't change, so reliable people are analogous to rocks.*

2. as quiet as a mouse (suggests an analogous relationship) _____

_____

3. Writing an essay is like building a house. (analogous to) _____

_____

4. Reality TV shows are like salted peanuts. (analogy between) _____

_____

G. Answer the questions using the target words in parentheses.

1. If you could meet Simon Colton, what would you ask him? (pose)
   I would pose a question about the future of his project.

2. How much can you study every day? (capacity)

_____

3. Do you know anything about intelligence testing? (notion)

_____

4. Do you think that robotic teachers would be a good idea? (notwithstanding)

_____

5. Do you think great art has one meaning or many meanings? (interpretation)

_____

Grammar | Reduced Adjective Clauses

Reduced adjective clauses are very common in writing. They make sentences shorter and clearer, and they also allow you to vary your writing. In a reduced adjective clause, the relative pronoun is deleted, causing the verb to change. There are three common ways to reduce an adjective clause:

1. Passive verbs and progressive verbs: Delete *be*.

   The museum holds some art ~~that is~~ painted by a robot.

2. *Be* as a main verb: Delete *be* from non-defining adjective clauses.

   Simon Colton, ~~who is~~ a computer scientist from Goldsmiths College, designed the software.

3. Most other verbs: Change the main verb to the *-ing* form.

       supporting
   These are all tools ~~that support~~ human creativity.

       resulting
   The software has generated realistic images from its knowledge of nature and art, ~~which results~~ in a wholly original but not very exciting canvas.

Adjective clauses should not be reduced if the verb tense is important or if there is a modal verb in the clause. Otherwise, some of the meaning will be lost.

   In the future, more powerful computers will run software *that might produce better art*.

   ✗ In the future, more powerful computers will run software *producing better art*.

The reduced clause omits the uncertainty of *might*.

A. Reduce the underlined clauses if possible. If you cannot reduce a clause, write ✗ above it.

1. Harold Cohen, ~~who is~~ a painter and professor of art, became interested in computer science when he moved to San Diego.

2. Cohen began to work in the field that is known as Artificial Intelligence (AI).

3. Scientists who were studying AI at Stanford University invited Cohen to join them in 1971.

4. Cohen and his colleagues studied the cognitive process of drawing, which resulted in a computer program called AARON.

5. AARON is software that can actually draw original artwork on paper.

6. Drawings that were made by AARON are exhibited in museums and science centers around the world.

B. Combine each pair of sentences by changing one of them to a reduced adjective clause.

1. The ability to see the world from a new perspective is a skill.
   The skill is called creativity.

   The ability to see the world from a new perspective is a skill called creativity.

2. Creative people see new things in familiar places.
   This leads to exciting new ideas.

   _____

3. Psychologists have studied successful business leaders.
   The psychologists are interested in creativity.

   _____

4. Andrew Grove says that businesses must "adapt or die!"
   Grove is the chairman of Intel.

   _____

5. Flexibility is the first characteristic.
   This characteristic is found in very creative leaders.

   _____

6. Creative businesspeople look for new experiences.
   These experiences open their minds to new possibilities.

   _____

C. Write a paragraph about a picture, photograph, painting, building, or public space that you like. Use reduced adjective clauses.

> *I once saw an amazing set of four photographs showing exactly the same scene in each of the four seasons. In spring there were leaves growing on the trees. The summer photograph, taken just after sunrise, is full of beautiful colors because the tree, surrounded by flowers, is in full bloom. In fall, my favorite season, ...*

_____

_____

_____

_____

_____

_____

WRITING SKILL   Paraphrasing

LEARN

Paraphrasing means "writing an author's idea in your own words." You need to paraphrase any time you summarize an article or another source in your writing. It is very important not to use the same words and sentences as the original article in your writing as this may be considered plagiarism.

To write a good paraphrase, follow these steps:

- Read the passage carefully and make sure you understand the ideas.

- Find similar words for most of the words in the original text.

- Keep keywords or words that have no good synonyms. Do not change them.

- Write sentences to express the author's ideas in your own words. Change the structure of the original sentences (e.g., active to passive voice or swap the dependent and independent clauses). Do not just replace words with synonyms.

- Put any exact phrases from the original in quotation marks.

APPLY

Read this sentence again from the magazine article on page 17. Complete the table and compare your answers with a partner. Which one is the best paraphrase?

"At first, [The Painting Fool] could only take existing photographs and apply different styles and techniques to produce an original piece."

Paraphrase	Is the information correct?	Is the sentence in the writer's own words?	Is this a good paraphrase?
1. Initially, the software could only take photographs and use different styles to produce an original artwork.			
2. The Painting Fool takes photographs and applies styles to them in order to make a new piece of art.			
3. In its early days, The Painting Fool created original art by combining photographic images using various artistic methods.			

Collaborative Writing

A. Read the paragraph carefully and underline the main ideas.

> *According to psychologists, immigrants are more creative than other people because they develop the capacity to see every situation from two radically different perspectives. Creativity requires a sense of discomfort. Therefore, children from comfortable backgrounds do not often work in creative industries.*

B. Which words can you use instead of these words and phrases from the paragraph? Work with a partner. Choose the best answer.

1. psychologists

   a. (scientists)   b. people   c. teachers

2. immigrants

   a. international visitors   b. children   c. people from other countries

3. develop the capacity

   a. struggle to adapt   b. learn the ability   c. are naturally capable

4. situation

   a. problem   b. experience   c. place

5. sense of discomfort

   a. unhappy experience   b. uncomfortable feeling   c. unpleasant thought

6. comfortable backgrounds

   a. wealthy families   b. poor households   c. developed countries

7. creative industries

   a. difficult jobs   b. the artistic sphere   c. interesting jobs

C. Complete the sentences to practice changing the structure of this sentence from the original paragraph: "Creativity requires a sense of discomfort."

1. A "sense of discomfort" _____*is required*_____ to be creative.

2. People need _____ in order to be creative.

3. Creative people _____.

D. Work with a partner. Summarize the ideas in the paragraph by paraphrasing them as in activity C, using words from activity B.

_____

_____

_____

_____

_____

_____

E. Compare your paraphrase with another pair's. Answer these questions together.

1. Does your paraphrase include all the important information?

2. Is the paraphrase in your own words?

3. How could you improve the paraphrase?

Independent Writing

A. You are going to write a summary and response. First, read the article _What Humans Know that Watson Doesn't_ on page 157. Write down three or four main ideas.

_____

_____

_____

_____

_____

_____

_____

B. In a summary and response, you often will give the other person's point of view and then provide your own thoughts on the topic. This is called "taking a stance." Answer the following questions.

1. Read the summary on page 18. Does the student writing the summary

   agree or disagree with the original author? _____

2. What language tells you that?

   _____

   _____

> **VOCABULARY TIP**
>
> When responding, use words and phrases like these to take a stance:
>
> _agree, be of the same mind as, claim, disagree with, doubt, prove, side with, question_

C. When you respond to an article, take a stance. Remember, your opinions need to relate to specific ideas in the article. What is your opinion about these ideas? Give a reason for each opinion.

1. Summary: Answering questions on a game show is not the same as dealing with real problems.

   Opinion: _____

   Reason: _____

   _____

2. Summary: The story of Watson is overhyped.

   Opinion: _____

   Reason: _____

   _____

3. Summary: Computers cannot have the same knowledge as humans because they cannot have human experiences.

   Opinion: _____

   Reason: _____

   _____

D. Discuss these questions with a partner. Take notes to use in your response to the article.

1. Which ideas in the article do you think are the most interesting, exciting, and useful?

2. Which ideas in the article do you think are disturbing, worrying, or uncomfortable?

3. Do you disagree with the writer on any points?

4. Do you have any experiences that relate to the ideas in the article?

E. Write a summary of the article in one paragraph followed by your response to the article in one or more paragraphs. Use your answers to activities A, C, and D to find and react to the main ideas. In your writing, use the target vocabulary words from page 15.

A. Read your summary and response. Answer the questions below, and make revisions as needed.

1. Check (✓) the information you included in your summary and response.

   ☐ main ideas from the article

   ☐ ideas you like or agree with

   ☐ reasons for each opinion in your response

   ☐ important supporting details from the article

   ☐ ideas you dislike or disagree with

2. Look at the information you did not include. Would adding that information make your summary and response better?

Grammar for Editing | **Defining versus Non-Defining Adjective Clauses**

A non-defining adjective clause adds extra information to the sentence:

> **Simon Colton, _who is a professor of computer science_, invented The Painting Fool.**

"who is a professor of computer science" adds extra information to the sentence. If we take the clause out of the sentence, it would still make sense. We use commas before and after non-defining clauses.

A defining adjective clause defines or restricts the noun to which it refers. If you removed the clause, you would not know exactly what the writer means.

> **The Painting Fool is a computer program _that creates original art_.**

> **Some paintings _that were created by computers_ are displayed in museums.**

The adjective clauses tell you what kind of program The Painting Fool is and which kind of paintings are displayed in museums.

B. Check the language in your summary and response. Revise and edit as needed.

Language Checklist
☐ I used target words in my summary and response.
☐ I used language to take a stance.
☐ I used reduced adjective clauses.
☐ I used defining and non-defining adjective clauses correctly.

C. Check your summary and response again. Repeat activities A and B.

Self-Assessment Review: Go back to page 15 and reassess your knowledge of the target vocabulary. How has your understanding of the words changed? What words do you feel most comfortable using now?

UNIT 3

A Powerful Force

In this unit, you will

> analyze a proposal and learn how it is used in the film industry.
> write a synopsis.
> increase your understanding of the target academic words for this unit.

WRITING SKILLS

> Writing a Proposal
> Writing a Synopsis
> **GRAMMAR** Gerunds and Infinitives

Self-Assessment

Think about how well you know each target word, and check (✓) the appropriate column. I have...

TARGET WORDS	never seen this word before.	heard or seen the word but am not sure what it means.	heard or seen the word and understand what it means.	used the word confidently in *either* speaking or writing.
AWL				
adjacent				
🔑 channel				
🔑 circumstance				
concurrent				
🔑 contemporary				
diverse				
framework				
ideology				
incorporate				
🔑 liberal				
🔑 revolution				
subsidy				
undertake				
🔑 via				

🔑 Oxford 3000™ keywords

Building Knowledge

Read these questions. Discuss your answers in a small group.

1. What is the most popular type of movie among your friends: drama, action, comedy, science fiction, or something else?

2. What is your favorite movie? What do you like about it?

3. A documentary is a film giving facts about a topic using interviews, news articles, videos, and other sources. What documentaries have you seen?

Writing Model

A proposal is used in schools, businesses, and the entertainment industry to explain an idea for a product or service. Read a proposal for a documentary film.

A Powerful Force

A Powerful Force explores the idealistic[1] beginnings of an international exchange program.

"The Fulbright Program aims to bring a
5 little more knowledge, a little more reason, and a little more compassion into world affairs and thereby increase the chance that nations will learn at last to live in peace and friendship."
—Senator J. William Fulbright

Senator Fulbright addressing an audience.

SYNOPSIS
10 Every year hundreds of thousands of young people leave home to study abroad or **undertake** a degree program at a foreign university. This is a life-changing experience, not only for the student, but for everyone the student encounters. The documentary *A Powerful Force* will trace this modern emphasis on international education back to the work of one
15 remarkable and idealistic politician, J. William Fulbright. Fulbright once said: "Education is a slow-moving but powerful force. It may not be fast enough or strong enough to save us from catastrophe, but it is the strongest force available." This documentary will show how Fulbright's own experience abroad led to the creation of a powerful force that continues to
20 change lives worldwide: the Fulbright Program.

---

[1] *idealistic:* believing in and trying to achieve perfect standards, even when it is not realistic

DESCRIPTION

A Powerful Force will be a documentary film about Fulbright's early inspiration and the creation of the Fulbright Program. This scholarship program has **subsidized** the work and study of a **diverse** group of students, teachers, and researchers since 1946. The **framework** for the film
25 is the life of Senator Fulbright. In spite of growing up in a time of war, he firmly believed that international peace and cooperation were possible.

The stories of two **contemporary** Fulbright alumni will also be **incorporated** into the documentary. Their stories will demonstrate the impact the program has had on people from **diverse** cultures and life
30 **circumstances** around the world. *A Powerful Force* will convince viewers of the lasting impact of human contact across borders. It will be shown in commercial theaters and on educational television **channels** around the world.

THE STORY

The movie opens in 1945 in Washington, D.C., a time of war. We see the
35 newly elected United States senators[2] taking their seats in the Senate. The senator from Arkansas has a name that will soon be associated with international cooperation. His name is J. William Fulbright. Within months of joining the Senate, Fulbright **undertakes** a project that will forever change international education. He writes a **revolutionary** legislative bill to
40 fund an exchange program. The scholarship promotes "international goodwill through the exchange of students in the fields of education, culture, and science." Politicians on both sides, **liberals** and conservatives, support the idea. Soon the bill is signed into law and the Fulbright Program is born.

45 At this point, the movie travels back in time. A map of the world zooms in to a small town in America's south in the late 1930s. The film shows how Fulbright grows up and matures into a natural leader at the University of Arkansas. Old photographs, newspaper articles, and interviews help to tell the story. The map again shows Fulbright's journey **via** ship across the
50 Atlantic Ocean to study at Oxford University in England. The film shows us how this scholarship experience transforms the young man's life. He returns home with a new appreciation for **diverse** cultures and a passion to enter public service as a politician. He also returns with the **ideology** that drives his political career: Living and studying in other countries help people
55 understand different points of view.

From here, the movie travels quickly forward in time, showing the incredible impact that this program has had around the world. Photos of some famous participants will be shown, using the world map to show where they studied. Clips[3] will include some of the 44 Nobel Prize winners who are
60 also Fulbright alumni,[4] as well as former presidents and prime ministers.

---

[2] *senators:* members of the Senate, which is the smaller group of legislators to which two people are elected from each state for a six-year term

[3] *clips:* short parts of a movie that are shown separately

[4] *alumni:* former members of a group, such as former students of a school, college, or university

Next we will meet two **contemporary** Fulbright winners. First, the film takes us to Arkhangelsk, Russia, where we meet Andrey Tikhonov. We follow Tikhonov as he is chosen
65 to be a foreign language teaching assistant at Michigan State University. During his time abroad, Tikhonov faces the typical linguistic and cultural challenges. He also faces physical challenges because he is blind. In the United
70 States, he learns how he can benefit from resources for disabled students. He begins to raise awareness about the issue of disability services on an international level. At Michigan State University, Tikhonov is a language instructor while **concurrently**
75 serving as a lecturer and concert violinist and pianist. He is a powerful example to the world that nothing can stop talent and that dreams can come true.

Andrey Tikhonov is from Arkhangelsk, Russia.

The next stop on the map is Mumbai, India. Environmental scientist Dr. Shubhalaxmi Vaylure is a participant in the Fulbright Indo-American
80 Environmental Leadership Program. At the University of Montana, she visits many nature education centers. When she returns to India, she begins to create similar projects there. She promotes conservation education for children and trains volunteers to protect the local environment. Through her international experience, she learns to bring her love of the natural
85 world back to her hometown and **adjacent** communities.

The film ends with images of Senator Fulbright with leaders and scholars around the world. The soundtrack[5] will include some of Fulbright's most important and inspiring quotations about international education. Through words and images, an international chorus of the world's most
90 promising scholars will join together into a "powerful force" for peace. In fact, as Fulbright says, it is "the most powerful force imaginable."

CONCLUSION

In our increasingly global world, international cooperation is more critical than ever. As former international students, the producers[6] are the ideal people to create a documentary showing the human impact of intercultural
95 exchange. The producers will capture the ongoing and vital importance of cross-cultural understanding through the Fulbright Program. ∎

---

[5] *soundtrack:* all the music, speech, and sounds that are recorded for a movie
[6] *producers:* people who are in charge of the practical and financial aspects of making a movie

LEARN

A movie proposal formally describes a plan for a film. The writer's goal is to persuade the reader to support or approve of the movie plan. Film producers submit proposals to film companies and investors in order to get money for the project.

Include these sections in a movie proposal:

1. Title and Concept. The title is typically followed by a one- or two-sentence concept description. An inspirational quotation is often placed after the title.

2. Synopsis. This is a one-paragraph summary of the proposed movie. It presents the main theme of the story and tells the story in general terms.

3. Description. This is a short description of the movie's genre, goal, and target audience, as well as the places where the movie will be shown. This section may also include background information about the topic.

4. The Story. This is a more detailed description of the proposed movie. The Story includes information about the characters in the movie and a narrative showing the sequence of events. The story is typically told using verbs in the present simple tense.

5. Conclusion. This is a short restatement of the theme of the movie. There may also be information about the producers of the movie.

APPLY

Read the statements below. In which section of the proposal on pages 32–34 does each item belong? Write the name of the section: *Title and Concept, Synopsis, Description, The Story, Conclusion.*

Description   1. It will be a full-length movie of about 100 minutes. It will be a motivational film for high school and college students.

_____   2. The film shows Fulbright's childhood in a small town in the late 1930s.

_____   3. It shows how the program continues to build international cooperation and understanding, using the strength of personal connections around the world.

_____   4. The producers will be able to use their network of Fulbright friends to locate captivating material for the documentary.

_____   5. *A Powerful Force* includes the inspiring stories of today's diverse participants and how they are changing the world.

Analyze

A. Complete the chart with information from the proposal.

1. Type of movie (genre)	*Documentary*
2. Theme or main idea of movie	
3. Time span (period of time that it will include)	

4. Main parts of the movie
 	
    a. Beginning
 	
    b. Middle
 	
    c. End	

5. Information about the producers	

B. Analyze the verb tenses that are used in the proposal. For each item below, find an example from the proposal. Circle the examples on pages 32–34 and write the line number below.

1. Simple present to express a general truth: *Line 10*

   Every year hundreds of thousands of young people leave home...

2. Simple present to tell the story as it happens: ___

3. Simple future to tell what the producers plan to do: ___

4. Future passive to show what will be done without naming who will do it: ___

5. Present perfect to show that something that happened in the past has a connection to the present: ___

C. Read the writing model again. Discuss these questions with a partner.

1. In a proposal, it is important to capture the reader's attention quickly at the beginning. What information captures your attention at the beginning?

2. Why do you think the writer included the profiles of the two Fulbright participants at the end? What purpose do they serve in the documentary?

3. What part of the movie do you think will be the most interesting? The least interesting? Explain your reasons.

4. If you were producing *A Powerful Force*, how would you change it? For example, would you present the contemporary Fulbright participants first? Would you include more alumni stories? Would you focus more on Senator Fulbright? Explain your answers.

Vocabulary Activities | STEP I: Word Level

Word Form Chart		
Noun	**Verb**	**Adjective**
diversity diversification	diversify	diverse

A. Complete the sentences with the correct form of the words from the chart. Use each word only once. Discuss the meaning of each sentence with a partner.

1. Tikhonov's talents are very _____ *diverse* _____ , ranging from languages to music.

2. At the University of Michigan, he enjoyed the _____ of the student body. He met students from all over the United States and the world.

3. Dr. Vaylure was able to _____ her skills, branching out from science into leadership, education, and management of nonprofit organizations.

4. The Fulbright Program encourages _____ of skills in its participants so that they can expand their talents and scholarship.

B. Complete the sentences with words from the box. You will use one word twice.

adjacent	circumstances	concurrently
framework	subsidy	via

1. Due to unforeseen _____, one of the producers was unable to attend the meeting.

2. The producers have developed a general _____ for their film proposal, but they have much more work to do to complete it.

3. Some of the details about the _____ leading up to Fulbright's election will not be included in the documentary.

4. The new theater is situated _____ to the park.

5. The theater received a _____ from the city to finance the new building.

6. Information about the grand opening is being sent _____ email.

7. There will be several workshops for teachers and actors happening

_____ on Saturday.

The noun *channel* has four different commonly used meanings.

1. a television station

2. a system that people use to communicate or to send something somewhere

   *Communication with the company president must go through the correct **channels**.*

3. a way of expressing your feelings or ideas or a way of using your energy or skills

   *Playing sports is a healthy **channel** for his competitive personality.*

4. a deep passage of water that connects two larger areas of water, used by ships

CORPUS

C. Complete the sentences with the correct form of the word *channel*. Write the meaning number (1–4) from the corpus box.

1. News about celebrities attending the Toronto Film Festival was carried on all of the major __*channels*__. Meaning: __1__

2. If you wish to schedule a TV interview with a film director there, you must go through the proper _____. Meaning: ____

3. One movie was about a man who decided to swim across the English _____, which separates England from France. Meaning: ____

4. Making dramatic movies is a great _____ for creative expression. Meaning: ____

Vocabulary Activities | STEP II: Sentence Level

As an adjective, *contemporary* means "modern or belonging to the same time period."

   *I watched a film about **contemporary** art from the mid-20th century.*

As a noun, *contemporary* means "a person who lives or who has lived during the same time as another person."

   *The actor was a **contemporary** of my father in college.*

CORPUS

D. Answer the questions. Use a form of *contemporary* in your answer.

1. Do you like to watch old movies? Explain your answer.

   I don't like old movies. Contemporary movies have more action.

2. Is there a very modern building or sculpture in your city?

_____

3. Who is a famous person that is the same age that you are?

_____

4. What are some current challenges facing students today?

_____

Word Form Chart			
Noun	**Verb**	**Adjective**	**Adverb**
ideology	_____	ideological	ideologically
incorporation	incorporate	incorporated	_____
liberal liberation	liberalize liberate	liberal	liberally
revolution	revolutionize	revolutionary	_____
undertaking	undertake	_____	_____

Note: The noun *undertaker* means "funeral director." It is not related to the word *undertaking*.

E. Rewrite the sentences using words from the word form chart. Change the verb tense as needed. Answers will vary. Compare your sentences with a partner.

1. At the beginning of the movie, the man was set free and he returned to his country.

   At the beginning of the movie, the man was liberated and he returned to his country.

2. The movie set has influences from contemporary art and industrial design.

   _____

3. The two filmmakers have very different belief systems.

   _____

4. The use of digital film techniques has resulted in many dramatic advances in film production.

   _____

5. Finding financial support for a movie proposal is a very time-consuming task.

   _____

6. The audience at the film festival tended not to be conservative in their political beliefs.

   _____

Grammar Gerunds and Infinitives

Some verbs can be followed by a gerund (verb + -ing) or an infinitive (to + verb). However, there is no clear guideline for deciding whether to use a gerund or an infinitive. You need to memorize which verbs are followed by gerunds, which are followed by infinitives, and which by either form.

Verbs followed by gerunds include the following: *avoid, consider, discuss, dislike, enjoy, finish, imagine, miss, practice, quit, recommend, resist, risk, suggest.*

> I *avoid seeing* horror films because they give me nightmares.

Verbs followed by infinitives include the following: *agree, appear, ask, attempt, be able, claim, decide, demand, expect, fail, hesitate, hope, intend, learn, need, offer, plan, prepare, promise, refuse, seem, volunteer, want, wish.*

> The producer *agreed to revise* the proposal.

Verbs followed by gerunds or infinitives include the following: *begin, continue, hate, like, love, prefer, start.*

> The viewer will *begin to appreciate* the vast impact of the Fulbright Program.

> The library will *begin charging* a fee for DVD rentals.

These verbs change meaning when followed by a gerund or by an infinitive: *forget, remember, stop, try.*

> I *remember locking* the door. (I know that I locked it this time.)

> I usually *remember to lock* the door. (In general, I lock my door.)

A. Complete the paragraph. Use the gerund or infinitive form of the verb in parentheses.

Muhammad Umar Anjum was working as a teaching and research associate

at a university in Lahore, Pakistan, when he first considered _____applying_____
(1. apply)

to the Fulbright Program. A professor asked him _____to think_____ about
(2. think)

applying for a position. Anjum felt that he knew little about the world

beyond his own country. He wanted _____to travel_____. He was accepted into
(3. travel)

the program and attended Michigan State University in the U.S. In addition

to taking classes related to his field, he was required _____to enroll_____ in
(4. enroll)

an American culture course. Anjum realized that Pakistan was not well

understood in the U.S. So, he volunteered _____to speak_____ about his country
(5. speak)

at local schools and libraries. By talking face to face with people from all

different backgrounds, he was able ___to open___ his own mind to new
(6. open)

understanding. Anjum says, "Wherever I go and whomever my students are,

I try ~~sharing~~ _to share_ with them what I have learned. I encourage them
(7. share)

___to be___ more open and ___to explore___ the world. I share with
(8. be)   (9. explore)

them that, for me, so many blinds were opened by traveling abroad and that

maybe they should do the same."

B. Correct the errors with gerunds or infinitives in the following sentences. Check
(✓) the sentences with no errors.

to become
___ 1. Anyone who wishes ~~becoming~~ a film director must love everything about
making movies.

producing
___ 2. For a young person, film experts recommend ~~to produce~~ short home
videos and editing them using computer software.

_✓_ 3. There is no standard channel for becoming a film director, but you should
attempt to acquire some formal training in the film industry.

gaining
___ 4. People will suggest ~~to gain~~ experience in a wide variety of settings such as
broadcasting, TV, theater, and advertising.

to start
___ 5. You can expect ~~starting~~ with many small jobs such as short commercials.

_✓_ 6. As a director, you will need the artistic creativity to manage film
production, actors, lighting, and design.

selecting.
___ 7. If you are not passionate about making films, you might consider ~~to select~~
a more realistic career goal. Successful directors are few in number.

C. Write sentences using the verbs below. Then share your sentences with a partner.

1. enjoy / discuss ___I enjoy discussing with my classmate___

2. be able / perform ___I'm able to perform on the stage___

3. avoid / watch ___I avoid watching her cry.___

4. stop / visit ___I___

5. fail / complete ___I fail to complete my homework.___

6. continue / study ___I continue study at school.___

7. volunteer / help ___I volunteer to help the others.___

WRITING SKILL Writing a Synopsis

LEARN

A synopsis is a special type of summary used for a movie or play. It gives only the major points or events, not the entire story (plot). The story is usually told in the present tense. A synopsis allows the reader to easily grasp what the movie is about.

In a movie proposal, the synopsis tells what the movie will be about. The functions of the synopsis in a movie proposal are

1. to quickly grab the reader's attention;

2. to present the main theme of the movie;

3. to introduce the main characters, without giving details; and

4. to make the reader want to learn more about the proposed movie.

APPLY

A. Reread the synopsis in the writing model on page 33. Discuss these questions with a partner.

1. Look at the following words and phrases from the synopsis. Which ones create interest? Which words make you curious to read more? Why?

catastrophe	life-changing experience	university
education	powerful	worldwide
hundreds of thousands	remarkable	

2. Which sentence gives the theme of the movie?

3. Which main character is introduced?

B. With a partner, arrange the sentences in order to create a synopsis for a future documentary. Then compare your answers with another group.

_____ 1. Forty-eight hours later, six of them are dead.

_____ 2. In August of 2011, 12 climbers reach the top of K2.

_____ 3. This thrilling story will leave viewers breathless as it shows an extreme battle of man against nature.

_____ 4. K2 is the most challenging and dangerous mountain in the world, attracting mountaineers from around the globe to climb its peak.

_____ 5. It will use actual video clips, interviews with survivors, and actors to tell the amazing story. The film will center on one man who risks his life to save his companions.

_____ 6. The documentary reveals the true story of that tragic day.

Collaborative Writing

A. In a small group, brainstorm topics for a documentary film. Choose a topic that will be interesting to a wide audience. Here are some possible topics: a famous person in history, a famous artist or performer, an important historical or contemporary event, an inspirational true story, or an interesting individual or place. Choose one topic for a documentary.

Documentary topic: _____

B. Use the documentary topic you chose in activity A. Develop the theme of your movie by answering these questions with your group.

1. What particular aspect of the person or event is most interesting to you? Why?

_____

2. What message or theme do you want your movie to communicate? How will your documentary do this?

_____

3. What events or situations will you focus on in order to convey your theme?

_____

C. Plan the synopsis for your movie proposal. Fill in the chart below.

1. Title and theme	
2. Main character(s) or event(s)	
3. Reason why this is an important or interesting topic	
4. Information about what will be in the movie, without too much detail	

D. Work with your group to write a one-paragraph synopsis of your movie proposal. Make sure you use the present tense to tell the events of the story, even if they happened in the past. Use the future to tell what effect your movie will have on the audience and what resources your movie will need.

E. Share your synopsis with another group. Discuss these questions.

1. Does the synopsis begin in an interesting way? How can it capture your audience's attention more quickly?

2. Is the topic something that many people will be interested in or can relate to?

3. Is there a clear statement of the theme of the movie?

4. Is the intention or purpose of the movie clear?

Independent Writing

A. You are going to create a movie proposal. First, think of a new movie to be the subject of your proposal. You can use the movie that you wrote a synopsis for in Collaborative Writing, or you can make up another one.

B. Write a detailed description of your movie for The Story section of your proposal. Divide your movie into three or four parts. Complete the chart below to organize important details.

Main characters: _____

  I. Part 1: _____

    Detail A: _____

    Detail B: _____

  II. Part 2: _____

    Detail A: _____

    Detail B: _____

  III. Part 3: _____

    Detail A: _____

    Detail B: _____

  IV. Part 4: _____

    Detail A: _____

    Detail B: _____

C. With a partner, discuss your outline. For each part of your movie, talk about what the audience will see (such as videos, photos, maps, and news articles). Think about how each visual element will carry the message of your movie. Write your ideas.

Visual elements, Part 1: _____

_____

Visual elements, Part 2: _____

_____

Visual elements, Part 3: _____

_____

Visual elements, Part 4: _____

_____

D. Write The Story part of your proposal, using your outline from activity B. Remember to tell the story in present tense, even though it happened in the past.

E. Complete these sentences about your movie proposal. Use vocabulary from the Vocabulary Tip box.

1. At the beginning, the film _____.

2. In this part, the movie will travel to _____, using

   _____ images of _____.

3. With _____ views of _____, the story

   _____.

4. At the end of the film, it _____, using _____

   views of _____.

> **VOCABULARY TIP**
>
> When describing a film, use these verbs to describe your goal for the film, or what the film will do:
>
> *capture, follow, lead us, move, show us, take us, travel*
>
> Use words like these to describe the types of images:
>
> *close-up, detailed, dramatic, panoramic, stunning, wide-angle*

F. Plan your writing for the Title and Concept, Description, and Conclusion. See page 34. Think about these questions:

1. Who will be the audience?

2. What are the title and main theme?

3. Why are you the best person to produce this film?

G. Write your complete proposal, putting together the sections. Use the target vocabulary words from page 31.

REVISE AND EDIT

A. Read your proposal. Answer the questions below, and make revisions to your proposal as needed.

1. Check (✓) the information you included in your proposal.

   ☐ title and brief description

   ☐ description with information about the film genre, theme, and audience

   ☐ brief conclusion, with information about the producer

   ☐ quotations

   ☐ synopsis

2. Look at the information you did not include. Would adding that information make your proposal better?

Grammar for Editing | Infinitives to Express Purpose

To express a purpose, use an infinitive. It is a shortened form of *in order to*. It answers the question "Why?"

> We will incorporate traditional music into the movie in order to create an authentic effect.

> *to + verb*
> We will incorporate traditional music into the movie <u>*to create*</u> an authentic effect.

Note that *for* can also be used to express purpose. It is followed by a noun, not a verb.

> *for + noun*
> We will incorporate traditional music into the movie <u>*for an authentic effect*</u>.

B. Check the language in your proposal. Revise and edit as needed.

Language Checklist
☐ I used target vocabulary in my proposal.
☐ I used the present tense in the synopsis and story sections of my proposal.
☐ I used gerund and infinitive verb forms correctly.
☐ I used infinitives to express purpose.

C. Check your proposal again. Repeat activities A and B.

Self-Assessment Review: Go back to page 31 and reassess your knowledge of the target vocabulary. How has your understanding of the words changed? What words do you feel most comfortable using now?

Music and Memory

In this unit, you will

> analyze fundraising letters and learn how they are used by charities.

> use persuasive writing to promote a charitable cause.

> increase your understanding of the target academic words for this unit.

WRITING SKILLS

> Supporting Ideas
> Developing Paragraphs
> **GRAMMAR** Parallel Form

Self-Assessment

Think about how well you know each target word, and check (✓) the appropriate column. I have…

TARGET WORDS	never seen this word before.	heard or seen the word but am not sure what it means.	heard or seen the word and understand what it means.	used the word confidently in *either* speaking or writing.
AWL				
advocate				
coincide				
conceive				
confine				
🔑 crucial				
induce				
levy				
practitioner				
🔑 promote				
reside				
sole				
trigger				
undergo				
welfare				

🔑 Oxford 3000™ keywords

Building Knowledge

Read these questions. Discuss your answers in a small group.

1. How do charities communicate with people when they want to ask for donations?

2. Have you or your family supported a charity? What kind of support did you give?

3. What information would persuade you to help a charity?

Writing Model

A fundraising letter is a letter or email sent by a charity or other nonprofit organization to raise money or ask readers to take a particular action. Read about one charity called Music and Memory.

Music and Memory

Dear Western State University Student:

Lou was a professor at this university for over 30 years. Although he taught chemical engineering, his real passion was for the jazz music he played with friends,
5 colleagues, and students. Now, Lou's a **resident** at the Bluebird Retirement Home, just steps away from campus. A recent stroke[1] **confined** him to his bed, and he cannot play his saxophone anymore. His speech is difficult to understand, and his short-term memory often fails him. But when he listens to classic
10 jazz on his MP3 player, his face **undergoes** a dramatic change. The music **triggers** emotions and feelings that take him back to his days playing with his own jazz band.

Lou's reaction is no **coincidence**. Music is profoundly linked to personal memories. In fact, our brains are hardwired to
15 connect music with long-term memory. For example, favorite music or songs associated with important personal events can **trigger** memories of lyrics[2] and of the experience connected to the music. Beloved music calms chaotic brain activity and enables the listener to focus on the present moment and regain
20 a connection to others. The benefits of this form of music therapy have been well studied and documented by distinguished researchers and **practitioners**. That's why we at Music and Memory are **advocating** for every **resident** like Lou in a long-term **residential** care facility to have access to a digital music player.

---

[1] *stroke:* a sudden serious brain illness, which can cause the loss of the ability to move or to speak clearly
[2] *lyrics:* the words of a song

Music and Memory was founded[3] by Dan Cohen. He **conceived** the idea in 2006
when he realized that none of the 16,000 nursing homes in the U.S. used personal music
players as part of their therapy. Extensive neuroscience research has shown how our
brains respond to music. In more than 60 Certified Music and Memory Care Facilities, our
personalized music system **levies** the therapeutic benefits of music for thousands of
residents. However, we can only continue our important mission with the help of you,
our supporters, which is why we are holding a donation[4] drive this week on your campus.

Your donation of a gently used MP3 player or a gift card to purchase music will
enable one more elderly or sick person to benefit from the healing powers of music. In
fact, access to a personalized playlist has been shown to **induce** dramatic improvements
in quality of life. This simple gift will provide pleasure, relaxation, and stimulation to
people who may otherwise feel isolated and alone. Individuals who listen to music are
less agitated,[5] need fewer medications, and are more cooperative with caregivers. The
research is clear: Music makes a **crucial** difference in long-term care facilities.

Here are some ways that you can help:
- Drop off your old music player at the Student Center between 4 p.m. and 8 p.m.
  any day this week.
- Buy a gift card for a digital music store and send it to "Music and Memory
  Donation Drive, Campus Box #5137" by the end of the month.
- **Promote** the campaign[6] to your friends by email and on social media.

You can play an amazing role in the lives of Lou and other **residents** at the Bluebird
Home. Music may be their **sole** connection with their pasts and the key to awaken
memories that will cheer and comfort them. Even though music players and digital
downloads are inexpensive, many long-term care facilities and other **welfare**
organizations are facing reduced budgets and cannot afford these items. We, as a campus,
can make sure that this simple, effective, and economical therapy is available to everyone
who could benefit from it. Without support from schools like ours, too many elderly
people could be trapped in a silent world.

Thank you for supporting the Music and Memory Donation Drive. You can find more
information about the charity on our website. You can also visit our table in the Student
Center any evening this week. Your gift of music will bring memory, pleasure, and
healing. Please give generously.

Sincerely,
Dave Adams
Campus Representative, Music and Memory

---

[3] *found:* to start something, such as an organization or an institution, especially by providing money
[4] *donation:* something that is given to a charity
[5] *agitated:* showing in your behavior that you are anxious and nervous
[6] *campaign:* a series of planned activities

WRITING SKILL | Supporting Ideas

LEARN

Writers of persuasive texts such as fundraising letters use a lot of supporting ideas to help persuade their readers to take some action. Supporting ideas can take many forms, depending on the type of writing, the topic, and the reader.

When you write a persuasive text, choose appropriate supporting ideas.

All persuasive writing	
• Examples (e.g., of people, events, actions, benefits, or problems) • Opinions of experts • Causes and effects	• Comparisons and contrasts • Historical details • Facts and statistics
Formal writing (e.g., academic essays)	**Less formal writing (e.g., campaign letters, newspaper articles, emails)**
• Research results • Quotations from books and articles	• Anecdotes and stories • Personal experiences

APPLY

A. Find one example of each type of support in the writing model on pages 48–49.

Type of support	Paragraph	Example
1. Anecdote or story	*1*	*Lou listening to music at the Bluebird Retirement Home*
2. Example		
3. Research result		
4. Historical detail		
5. Cause/effect		
6. Statistics		

B. Which of these sentences could be added to the letter? Where could they be inserted? Write the paragraph number or *N/A* if the sentence is not useful supporting information. Discuss your answers with a small group.

_1_ 1. Lou's children live hundreds of miles away, so he is often lonely.

____ 2. For example, music therapists often use music from patients' childhood to calm them when they become stressed or frustrated.

____ 3. MP3 players first became popular in the early 2000s.

____ 4. You can also learn more about the work of Music and Memory by contacting the Bluebird Home—volunteers are always welcome!

____ 5. Neuroscientists have found that music triggers parts of the brain that are otherwise totally inactive in elderly or sick people.

Analyze

A. Read the fundraising letter again and put the stages of the letter in the correct order.

___ 1. Explain what and how to donate.

___ 2. Thank the reader and offer more information.

_1_ 3. Attract the reader's attention with a powerful story.

___ 4. Introduce the organization.

___ 5. Describe how the reader's donation will benefit the organization's work.

___ 6. Show the negative consequences if readers don't take action.

B. Find examples in the letter of these ways of persuading an audience. Make notes in the table.

Appeals to the reader's emotions	1. *The story about Lou*
	2. _____
Logical arguments	3. _____
	4. _____
Support from experts and other authorities	5. _____
	6. _____
The importance of acting quickly	7. _____
	8. _____

C. Discuss these questions with a partner or small group.

1. Why does the writer thank readers for supporting the drive before they have made a donation?

2. What would be the effect of starting the letter in these ways rather than with the story of Lou? Would the letter still be persuasive?

   a. the request for donations

   b. the history of the charity

   c. the negative effects of not supporting the campaign

3. Why do you think the writer includes the results of neuroscientific research? Would you write this letter differently if it weren't for a university audience?

4. What language features of the letter would be inappropriate for an academic persuasive essay?

Vocabulary Activities STEP I: Word Level

A. Complete the sentences with the correct words from the box. Do not use any word more than once. You will not use two of the words.

coincided	crucial	levied	trigger
confined	induced	sole	undergone

1. The benefits of music are not _____ to the sick and elderly.

2. It is _____ to support charities that help people in need.

3. Our organization is the _____ provider of healthcare services in the village.

4. Music can _____ happy or sad memories.

5. Fundraising has _____ a major change because of social media.

6. The government has _____ a new tax to pay for care of the elderly.

7. With a good fundraising letter, readers can be _____ to take action.

The noun *welfare* has three different meanings.

1. the general health or well-being of a person, animal, or group

   *The organization works to protect <u>children's **welfare**</u>.*

2. help provided, often by a government, to people in need

   *The money is used to fund <u>social **welfare** programs</u> in developing countries.*

   *<u>**Welfare** services</u> are provided by local governments and other agencies.*

3. money given regularly by the government to people who are poor, unemployed, or too sick to work

   *After Susan lost her job, she had to live <u>on **welfare**</u>.*

   CORPUS

B. Write the word *welfare* in the four sentences where it can be correctly used. Write ✗ if it cannot. Discuss the meaning of each sentence with a partner.

1. We are working to protect the _____ of the whales and dolphins.

2. You can help by giving money, time, or _____.

3. It can be very difficult to live on _____.

4. The charity supports _____ programs in the local community.

5. The government's responsibility is to _____ its people.

6. Improving the environment is beneficial to the general _____.

C. Rewrite the sentences using the target vocabulary in parentheses. Change the form if necessary.

1. People who live in long-term-care homes are sometimes lonely. (residents)

   Loneliness is a common problem for residents of long-term-care homes.

2. I can imagine that disabled children would benefit from music therapy. (conceivably)

3. The fundraising campaign happened at the same time as a newspaper article about the charity. (coincided)

4. Places with lots of houses may have many hidden social problems. (residential)

5. The man opened his eyes when the music played, but perhaps it was just an unrelated incident. (coincidental)

6. The cost of providing disaster relief is unimaginably high. (inconceivably)

D. Write sentences to answer the questions. Use the target words in parentheses.

1. Is it important to do charity work or donate to charities? (crucial)

2. How can professionals, such as teachers and doctors, donate their time to benefit others? (practitioner)

3. Do you believe that charities should be limited to supporting local projects, or should they work around the globe? (promote)

4. If you could donate to only one charity, what would it be? (sole)

5. Has your local community experienced any changes in the last ten years? (undergo)

Advocate is a noun and a verb. As a noun, it can mean "a supporter of someone or something." A common collocation is *staunch advocate*, meaning "a strong and consistent supporter."

> We are **advocates** <u>for</u> the rights of elderly patients.

> She is an **advocate** <u>of</u> teaching music in schools.

As a verb, *advocate* means "to support something publicly." The preposition *for* is sometimes used.

> We strongly **advocate** the use of music as part of therapy.

> Music and Memory **advocates** (for) providing personal music players in long-term-care homes.

CORPUS

E. Write two sentences using the words provided and both the noun form and the verb form of *advocate*. Add prepositions if necessary.

1. The World Wildlife Fund / endangered animals

   The World Wildlife Fund is an advocate for endangered animals.

   The World Wildlife Fund advocates for endangered animals.

2. Habitat for Humanity / building homes for poor families

   _____

   _____

3. Doctors Without Borders / disease prevention in developing countries

   _____

   _____

4. The Gates Foundation / the use of educational technology

   _____

   _____

Grammar | Parallel Form

Lists of two or more adjectives, nouns, verbs, or phrases can be very effective in persuasive writing. In these lists, each item must have the same grammatical form. This is called parallel form.

nouns

✓ He played with <u>friends</u>, <u>colleagues</u>, and <u>students</u>.

infinitives

✓ Music enables the listener to <u>focus</u> on the present moment and <u>regain</u> a connection to others.

Sentences that are not parallel are awkward to read or may be ungrammatical.

infinitive   gerund

✗ Music enables the listener to <u>focus</u> on the present moment and <u>regaining</u> a connection to others.

A. Read these sentences. Underline the lists. Make changes to make the lists parallel.

reduce

1. Music can <u>trigger happy memories, calm frustrated feelings, and reducing anxiety.</u>

2. MP3 players provide comfort, pleasure, and relaxing.

3. You can support the organization by making a donation, volunteering your time, or to make phone calls.

4. Our charity helps people who have disabilities, the sick, and the elderly.

5. After a natural disaster, charities help victims physically, emotionally, and with money.

B. Circle the correct words and phrases in parentheses to make the lists parallel.

There are two types of memory: long-term and short-term memory. Long-term memory is the store of knowledge, events, and (1) (experiences / experiencing) from the past. Many experts believe that these memories are organized like a filing cabinet. Each topic has a folder, so every time you learn something new, you either add to an existing folder or (2) (create / creating) a new one. Most people can keep information in their long-term memories for a long period of time. This explains why you can remember scenes from your childhood and (3) (facts from your school days / learning facts in school).

Short-term memory, on the other hand, is temporary and (4) (limit / limited). On average, it is possible to remember seven items, (5) (vocabulary / words), or numbers. For example, in many countries telephone numbers are six or seven digits long and (6) (you can easily remember them / can be easily remembered). Together, these two types of memory allow us to learn and retain a lifetime of information and experiences.

C. **Complete the sentences. Make sure the lists are parallel.**

1. A good fundraising letter is clear, direct, and ___*persuasive*___.

2. I support charities that help sick children, support scientific research, and

   _____.

3. After a natural disaster, you should donate food, clothing, or _____.

4. Charities reach donors by sending letters, making phone calls, and

   _____.

5. Music, art, and _____ can provide therapy to the sick and elderly.

D. **Combine each pair of sentences into one sentence. Use the conjunction in parentheses.**

1. People who have certain illnesses can lose their memory. Other people who have brain injuries can also lose their memory. (or)

   People who have certain illnesses or brain injuries can lose their memory.

2. Amnesia (memory loss) can affect long-term memory. In other cases, it can affect short-term memory. (or)

   _____

3. Short-term amnesia damages the ability to remember new information. However, it preserves long-term memory. (but)

   _____

4. Amnesiac patients keep their intellectual skills. They also keep their social skills. (and)

   _____

5. Learning new memory strategies is a successful treatment for some patients with amnesia. Patients can also use digital devices. (and)

   _____

WRITING SKILL   Developing Paragraphs

LEARN

In most academic and formal writing, each paragraph fully develops one idea. This means a paragraph must be several sentences long—although good writers vary the lengths of their paragraphs. One-sentence paragraphs are common in fiction and newspaper writing, where they are used for effect, but are not usually allowed in academic writing. A well-developed paragraph has the following characteristics:

- It is about one topic or main idea only. (This is called unity.)

- It has smooth, logical connections between sentences. (This is called cohesion.)

- It does not repeat any ideas.

- It has enough support to develop the main idea.

The first sentence of a paragraph often creates a transition from the previous paragraph and introduces the topic of the current one.

APPLY

Read the second paragraph of the writing model on page 48 again. Discuss these questions with a partner.

1. What is the topic or main idea of the paragraph?

2. Which sentence in the paragraph is most clearly connected to the topic of the first paragraph?

3. Which words in each sentence make a logical connection to the previous sentence?

4. Are any ideas repeated?

5. Is there enough support to develop the main idea?

Collaborative Writing

A. Read the paragraph. Then complete the chart below.

> Music for Schools is a charity that provides musical instruments for schoolchildren. Violins are the most common instruments for young learners. Learning an instrument teaches children about hard work, concentration, and pattern recognition. Music for Schools works to bring instruments to schools. Playing music is good for all children. Please support Music for Schools.

Question	Yes/No	Why, or why not?
1. Does the paragraph have unity?		
2. Are all the sentences logically and smoothly connected?		
3. Are any ideas repeated?		
4. Is there enough support to develop the main idea?		

B. Work with a partner. Rewrite the paragraph in activity A.

1. Choose one of these sentences to start your paragraph.

   a. Can you give a child the gift of music?

   b. Learning an instrument is beneficial for children, but it can also be very expensive.

   c. Music for Schools needs your support to bring musical instruments to your local school.

2. Brainstorm supporting ideas (examples, personal experiences, interesting details, causes and effects, and other specific information).

   _____

   _____

   _____

3. Now write the paragraph. Connect your sentences and avoid repetition.

C. Share your new paragraph with another pair. Answer these questions about each paragraph.

1. Does the paragraph have unity?

2. Are all the sentences logically and smoothly connected?

3. Are any ideas repeated?

4. Is there enough support to develop the main idea?

Independent Writing

A. Imagine you want to persuade your classmates to support a fundraising or donation campaign by writing a letter. What cause or charity would you want people to support? Answer the questions below.

1. Make a list of charities or causes that you know about or that you can imagine. Write down ideas for campaigns for them.

Causes and charities	Fundraising or donation campaigns

2. Discuss your ideas with a partner. Choose the best one.

B. Complete the chart with supporting information about the idea you chose in activity A that you could include in a persuasive letter.

1. Story to attract the reader's attention	
2. Reasons why your cause is important	
3. Specific information about how your readers can help	
4. Negative consequences if readers don't act	

C. Complete the sentences with a strong adjective. Use a dictionary or thesaurus to help you.

1. The quality of food in our hospital is _____awful_____.

2. Pollution in the local environment is _____.

3. There is a(n) _____ need for warm clothing.

4. You can make a(n) _____ difference in the life of your community.

5. Without your help, the situation will become _____.

> **VOCABULARY TIP**
>
> Use strong adjectives to persuade your reader that your cause is important and that they can make a real difference. For example, say that the situation is *urgent* or *desperate* or the work of your charity is *vital*, *essential*, or *crucial*.

D. Write a fundraising letter. Use the ideas and supporting information from activities A and B and adjectives from activity C. Use the target vocabulary words from page 47.

A. Read your fundraising letter. Answer the questions below, and make revisions as needed.

1. Check (✓) the information you included in your letter.

☐ interesting story   ☐ information about the cause or charity

☐ supporting details

☐ negative consequences   ☐ how readers can help

                                                  ☐ thanks to the reader

2. Look at the information you did not include. Would adding that information make your letter more persuasive to readers?

Grammar for Editing | Pronouns

1. Pronouns must match the nouns to which they refer.

                                                    their

    Charities have to communicate effectively with <u>its</u> supporters.

2. Be careful not to use *he* or *she* to mean everyone. It is often easier to use plurals.

    ✗ Every patient can have <u>his</u> own personal music player.

    ? Every patient can have <u>his or her</u> own personal music player.

    ✓ All patients can have <u>their</u> own personal music players.

3. Use object pronouns for direct and indirect objects.

                  them

    You can give <u>they</u> the gift of music.

4. Possessive pronouns are determiners. Don't use articles with them.

    This is ~~the~~ <u>your</u> chance to help.

B. Check the language in your fundraising letter. Revise and edit as needed.

Language Checklist
☐   I used target words in my fundraising letter.
☐   I used strong adjectives.
☐   I used parallel form.
☐   I used pronouns correctly.

C. Check your letter again. Repeat activities A and B.

Self-Assessment Review: Go back to page 47 and reassess your knowledge of the target vocabulary. How has your understanding of the words changed? What words do you feel most comfortable using now?

UNIT 5

R U Txting in Class?

In this unit, you will

> analyze scientific writing and learn how it is used in a research paper.

> use narrative, process, and analytical writing to report on your research.

> increase your understanding of the target academic words for this unit.

WRITING SKILLS

> Old-New Information Patterns
> Summarizing Data
> **GRAMMAR** Passive Voice

Self-Assessment

Think about how well you know each target word, and check (✓) the appropriate column. I have...

TARGET WORDS	never seen this word before.	heard or seen the word but am not sure what it means.	heard or seen the word and understand what it means.	used the word confidently in *either* speaking or writing.
AWL				
aggregate				
constrain				
empirical				
incentive				
inherent				
inhibit				
integral				
intrinsic				
norm				
phenomenon				
qualitative				
🔑 sex				
underlie				
🔑 whereas				

🔑 Oxford 3000™ keywords

Building Knowledge

Read these questions. Discuss your answers in a small group.

1. Do you or your friends use cell phones in class? When and how do you use them?

2. Do you think it is possible to do two things well at the same time?

3. Have you ever done a research project? What did you find?

Writing Model

A research paper is an article in an academic journal that describes the results of an experiment. Read the excerpt from a paper from the *Journal of Marketing Education* about students who send text messages from their cell phones during class.

THE IMPACT OF TEXTING ON STUDENTS IN MARKETING CLASSES

Dennis E. Clayson and Debra A. Haley
Journal of Marketing Education, Vol. 35, Issue 1 (April 2013)

Introduction

The motivation for this study began with an incident in class that has become increasingly common. One of the authors noted that several students were looking intently down at their laps

5 and texting during a lecture. The instructor stopped and made a number of comments about texting in class, explaining that it was a sign of disrespect for the instructor and the other students. Furthermore, business students should

10 be aware that texting under these conditions would be considered unprofessional. The students appeared to accept the information, but within minutes several students had begun texting again.

15 Texting has become so **integral** to student life that they simply text even if it is against the rules. Texting in class concerns many instructors, and a number of approaches have been attempted to control this behavior. Some

20 instructors have appealed to good manners (Goodwin, 2012). Other professors have used the **incentive** of grades, **whereas** others have tried punishments. Evidently, these attempts to control texting in class have been largely

25 ineffective (Williams et al., 2011).

The problem **inherent** with multitasking in class is that learning requires substantial cognitive[1] processing (Mayer & Moreno, 2003). However, when students are texting, their

30 ability to learn is severely **inhibited**. This is because these students' brains are receiving information in two different ways: sound (the lecturer's voice) and vision (the words on their screens). However, when students are listening

---

[1] *cognitive:* connected with mental processes of understanding

and reading at the same time, a bottleneck[2] can occur. This slows down learning like a construction project on a busy highway. Therefore, multitasking has a negative effect on attention. In other words, students' brains cannot concentrate on the content of the class if they are also texting (Gorlick, 2009).

The purpose of this **empirical** study is to investigate the texting **phenomenon** in marketing classes, specifically by addressing two basic questions:

Research Question 1: How much do marketing students text?

Research Question 2: Does texting behavior influence grades?

Methods

Data were collected during the spring and summer terms of 2011 and 2012 at two universities. Students in marketing classes volunteered to fill out a questionnaire about their texting habits. The total number of students who completed the survey was 298, with approximately equal numbers of both **sexes**. The survey was designed to cover a wide range of behaviors and attitudes about texting. For each student, the grade received in the class was also recorded.

Results

A summary of the results can be found in Table 1. Only 2% of the students had not texted anyone during the semester. The **aggregate** number of texts received per day was 37, and students sent slightly fewer than 16. Interestingly, as many as 94% of the students received texts while in a class, and 86% texted while in class.

The majority of students denied being compulsive[3] about texting. More than two-thirds thought that they could text and follow a lecture at the same time, and only 29% thought that texting would influence their grades. However, almost half (42%) thought it was reasonable to ban texting in class. As can be seen in Figure 2, texting in classes resulted in a significant decrease in class grade (80% for texters versus 87% for non-texters). Non-texters also had slightly higher overall GPAs.[4]

Discussion

These results have important implications for teaching. The students strongly deny that they are addicted to texting, yet almost all of them texted someone while in class. Furthermore, even though the majority of

Question	Yes	No
Did you send or receive texts during the semester?	98%	2%
Did you text someone in class?	86%	14%
Did you receive texts in class?	94%	6%
Did you have a professor who banned texting in class?	56%	46%
Can you text and follow a lecture at the same time?	47%	32%
Is it reasonable to ban texting?	42%	36%
Are you addicted to texting?	11%	75%
Do you think texting during class affects your grades?	29%	47%
	Average number	
How many texts did you send every day?	15.5	
How many texts did you receive every day?	37.3	
How many texts do you receive in every class?	2.9	
How many texts do you send in every class?	2.6	

Figure 1: Survey results of texting behavior

---

[2] *bottleneck:* anything that delays development or progress
[3] *compulsive:* not being able to control their behavior
[4] *GPA:* grade point average (the average of a student's grades over a period of time)

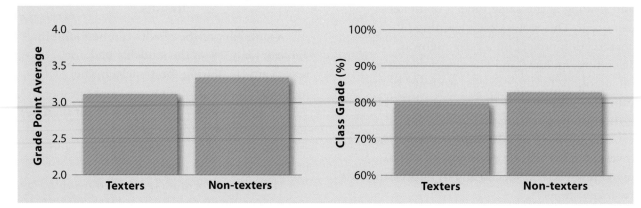

Figure 2: Overall GPA and class grade for texters and non-texters

students agreed that they should not text in class, about half did so anyway.

One likely interpretation is that classroom **norms** have changed as culture and technology have changed. The classroom has become more informal. However, this change has an important disadvantage. Neuroscience research offers strong evidence that texting **inhibits** learning. Indeed, in this study, texters received lower grades in class. Yet our results and the literature seem to suggest that texting in class cannot be stopped using traditional **constraints**.

This study does not reveal why students choose to text in class. Only further **qualitative** research will reveal these reasons. However, research has shown that marketing students can and do choose their level of effort based on their **underlying** educational goals (Taylor, Hunter, Melton, & Goodwin, 2011). Students who are **intrinsically** motivated will think more deeply than students with extrinsic motivation. Others can be given motivation through engaging classroom activities. Texting may be here to stay. However, educating students on when it is appropriate to text and providing them with an engaging classroom will be better for everyone.

References

Goodwin, M. (2012, Nov 12). Manners in the syllabus. *The Chronicle of Higher Education*. Retrieved from http://chronicle.com/blogs/brainstorm/manners-in-the-syllabus/36409

Gorlick, A. (2009, Aug 24). Media multitaskers pay mental price. *Stanford Report*. Retrieved from http://news.stanford.edu/news/2009/august24/multitask-research-study-082409.html

Mayer, R. E., & Moreno, R. (2003). Nine ways to reduce cognitive load in multimedia learning. *Educational Psychologist, 38*(1), 43–52.

Taylor, S. A., Hunter, G. L., Melton, H., & Goodwin, S. A. (2011). Student engagement and marketing classes. *Journal of Marketing Education, 33*(1), 73–92.

Williams, J. A., Berg, H., Gerber, H., Miller, M., Cox, D., Votteler, N., & McGuire, M. (2011). "I get distracted by their being distracted": The etiquette of in-class texting. *Eastern Educational Journal, 40*(1), 48–56.

LEARN

An important method for creating cohesion when developing a paragraph is to use old-new information patterns. This means that the first (new) part of a sentence (usually the subject) is linked to the (old) information in the previous sentence. Look at the example below. The colors represent the same ideas.

Texting has become so integral to student life that they simply text even if it is against the rules. Texting in class concerns many instructors, and a number of approaches have been attempted to control this behavior. Some instructors have appealed to good manners. Other professors have used the incentive of grades, whereas others have tried punishments. Evidently, these attempts to control texting in class have been largely ineffective.

When you use old-new information patterns, follow these steps:

- Repeat keywords and ideas from previous sentences in the subject.

- Use words such as *some, another, other,* and *the first/second/third* to create lists.

- Use *this* or *these* as pronouns or determiners or the article *the* to refer back to previous ideas.

APPLY

A. Read this paragraph again from the research paper. Then answer the questions.

[1]The problem inherent with multitasking in class is that learning requires substantial cognitive processing. [2]However, when students are texting, their ability to learn is severely inhibited. [3]This is because these students' brains are receiving information in two different ways: sound (the lecturer's voice) and vision (the words on their screens). [4]However, when students are listening and reading at the same time, a bottleneck can occur. [5]This slows down learning like a construction project on a busy highway. [6]Therefore, multitasking has a negative effect on attention. [7]In other words, students' brains cannot concentrate on the content of the class if they are also texting.

1. What does *this* mean in Sentence 3? _____

2. What is the old information in Sentence 4?

_____

3. What does *this* mean in Sentence 5? _____

4. Which word in Sentence 6 repeats the idea "when students are listening and reading at the same time"?

_____

5. What is the purpose of Sentence 7?

_____

B. Put these sentences in the best order to form a complete paragraph using old-new information structure.

___ 1. First, looking at a cell phone or radio button, even briefly, takes the driver's eyes off the road.

_1_ 2. Many people believe they can do another task while driving.

___ 3. If a driver loses concentration just for a short time, a serious accident can happen.

___ 4. This can cause the driver to make a mistake.

___ 5. This means that people who text or make phone calls cannot concentrate fully on their driving.

___ 6. Because of the increase in accidents, new laws have been made that restrict the use of cell phones in cars.

___ 7. The second reason is that the brain cannot process two sets of information at the same time.

___ 8. However, multitasking behind the wheel is dangerous for two reasons.

Analyze

A. Where do you find this information in a research report? Write *I* for Introduction, *M* for Methods, *R* for Results, or *D* for Discussion.

_I_ 1. Research questions

___ 2. Answers to the research questions

___ 3. Summary of previous research

___ 4. Summary of the data

___ 5. Description of the survey and the participants

___ 6. Reasons for doing the research

___ 7. Implications of the research

___ 8. Interpretations of the data

B. Complete the chart. Write the verb tenses that are used in each section of the research paper. Give the reason that each verb tense is used.

Section	Verb form	Reason
Introduction	Past simple	Tell a story about the professor's class
	Present simple	Describe the current situation of students texting in class
	Present perfect	
Methods		
Results		
Discussion		

C. Discuss these questions with a small group.

1. Why didn't the authors use "we" in the first paragraph when they described an incident in class?

2. Why are there many citations near the end of the introduction section?

3. Why are there also citations in the discussion section?

4. Why are there so many passive verbs in the methods section?

Vocabulary Activities | STEP I: Word Level

A. Complete the paragraph using words from the box. Do not repeat any word. You will not use two of the words.

aggregates	inhibited	norms	qualitative	underlie
constraints	integral	phenomenon	sexes	whereas

According to a recent (1) _____ research study, there are

differences between the (2) _____ in texting behavior. Although

texting is (3) _____ to the social lives of both genders, women

write messages with more expressive language than men, who are somewhat

more (4) _____ in their texts. (5) _____ women wrote

longer messages, they also used more abbreviations. This may be due to the

(6) _____ of text messaging (the length of a message is limited),

but other differences in communication style may (7) _____

these results. Overall, it seems that two separate (8) _____ are

developing for the use of texting.

Inherent, integral, and *intrinsic* all have a similar meaning: "a basic, essential, or permanent part of something." However, they collocate with different nouns.

> **intrinsic** + motivation / value / nature / worth / interest / meaning
> **integral** + part / component / role / element / aspect
> **inherent** + problem / risk / danger / power / right / limitation / difficulty / conflict

Intrinsic is used with the meaning of "internal" and often has a positive sense.

> *Successful language learners have **intrinsic** motivation.*

Integral is used with the meaning of "an essential part of a whole."

> *Peer review is an **integral** part of the scientific method.*

Inherent often means that "someone is born with quality or right." However, it often also means that "a problem or difficulty naturally exists."

> *There are **inherent** problems with survey research.*

CORPUS

B. **Complete the sentences with your own ideas. Compare your answers with a partner.**

1. An inherent limitation to text messages is _____

2. An intrinsic value of texting is _____

3. An inherent risk of texting while driving is _____

4. An integral aspect of the popularity of texting is _____

Vocabulary Activities STEP II: Sentence Level

C. **Write sentences about a research study with which you are familiar. Use the target phrases. Compare your sentences with a partner.**

1. qualitative study *This paper reports on a qualitative study of laptop use in class.*

2. the phenomenon of _____

3. empirical evidence _____

4. incentive for participation _____

5. the aggregate number of _____

6. whereas _____

Constrain has the basic meaning of *limit*, but it is used in formal contexts.

1. To mean "limit something," often in the passive voice:

   *Further research <u>was</u> **constrained** by a lack of resources.*

2. To mean "prevent someone from doing something," also often in the passive:

   *We <u>are</u> **constrained** <u>from</u> providing more details by privacy concerns.*

3. To mean "force someone to do something in a particular way":

   *Some professors feel **constrained** <u>to</u> restrict the use of technology even when it could be beneficial.*

The noun *constraint* is usually plural, with meaning of "limits, difficulties, or restriction."

   *Due to financial **constraints**, class sizes will increase next year.*

   *A ban on laptops would <u>impose serious</u> **constraints** <u>on</u> students with learning difficulties.*

An exception is the phrase *without constraint*, which means without restrictions.

   *You are free to write <u>without</u> **constraint** on the class discussion board.*

CORPUS

D. Answer these questions using a form of the words *constrain* and *constraint*.

1. What limits should teachers put on cell phones in class?

   _____

   _____

2. Should teenagers be allowed to use cell phones without any restrictions?

   _____

   _____

3. As a child, what were you not allowed to do?

   _____

   _____

4. What do you not have enough time or money to do now?

   _____

   _____

5. What happens to students in your school who fail a class?

   _____

   _____

Grammar | Passive Voice

The passive voice is common in scientific and other academic writing. It's especially used in the following situations.

1. to avoid agents (subjects) that are not known, are obvious, are not important, or are very general;

   general subject
   ✗ <u>People</u> send billions of text messages every day.
   ✓ Billions of text messages <u>are sent</u> every day.

2. to make old information the subject of the sentence (This improves cohesion.);

   ✗ There are <u>two channels</u> of input to the brain. Texting and listening to a lecture use <u>both channels</u>.
   ✓ There are <u>two channels</u> of input to the brain. <u>Both channels</u> <u>are used</u> when texting and listening to a lecture.

3. to describe the methodology of a research study; and

   The research <u>was carried out</u> at three universities.

4. to avoid using *I, you,* or *we.*

   ✗ <u>You</u> can see the results in Table 1.
   ✓ The results <u>can be seen</u> in Table 1.

A. Write sentences about a research study in the passive voice, using the words given. Choose the correct tense.

1. A recent study / conduct / laptop use in class

   A recent study was conducted on laptop use in class.

2. Participants / show / 45-minute lecture

   _____

3. The students / ask / to take notes on their laptops

   _____

4. Half the students / tell / to multitask while listening

   _____

5. Lower comprehension grades / receive / the multitasking students

   _____

6. Students sitting behind the multitaskers / also / distracted

   _____

B. Choose the correct form of the verbs in parentheses.

Successful college students (1) (use / are used) strategies that help them study better, not harder. Previous research (2) (studied / was studied) students' use of strategies such as self-testing and rereading. However, the effect of these strategies on students' grades (3) (did not investigate / was not investigated). Therefore, Hartwig and Dunlosky (2012) (4) (conducted / were conducted) a study to see whether strategic students earn better grades. Over 300 students (5) (surveyed / were surveyed) about their use of strategies such as making a schedule, rereading their notes, and testing themselves before quizzes. The students' grades (6) (collected / were collected). The researchers (7) (found / were found) that students who used some of the strategies (8) (received / were received) higher grades. However, studying all night (9) (linked / was linked) to lower grades. Therefore, if students (10) (teach / are taught) good study habits early, they should be more successful.

C. Read the following paragraph and change five of the verbs to the passive voice to make it more academic and cohesive. Write the new sentences below.

Multitasking is not actually possible. People cannot really do two tasks at the same time. Therefore, you should call multitasking "task switching." Task switching is inefficient because the brain needs time to switch between tasks. You can lose one-tenth of a second on each switch. When you add up all those short delays, there is a large effect on productivity. Task switching wastes up to 40% of productivity. Therefore, efficient workers learn to do one thing at a time instead of task switching.

1. *Two tasks cannot really be done at the same time.*

2. multitasking should be called "task-switching".

3. One-tenth of a second can be lost.

4. When all those short days are add up...

5. up to 40% of productivity is wasted.

WRITING SKILL   Reporting Data

LEARN

The results and discussion sections of a research paper usually require you to report on and analyze data. The data might be numbers, calculations, observations, or interviews. The strategy for writing these sections is similar:

- Refer the reader to tables or charts, if applicable.

- Explain what the charts show.

- Highlight the most important data. Do not repeat every piece of data.

- Use words such as *a majority, only, nearly,* and *almost* to help the reader interpret the data.

- Describe patterns and trends in the data (*the number of students is rising; the cost of computers has fallen; sales of this product have remained stable*).

- Include your explanations and interpretations of the data in the discussion section, not the results.

APPLY

A. Look again at the results section of the research paper on pages 62–64. Are the following statements true or false? Why?

1. (T)/ F The number of students who did not text during the semester was small.

   Why? _The writers say that "only" 2% had not texted, which means they think the_

   number is small.

2. T / F A surprising number of students sent or received texts in class.

   Why? _____

3. T / F A large number of students thought texting would affect their grades.

   Why? _____

4. T / F A lot of students thought teachers could reasonably ban texting in class.

   Why? _____

B. Look again at the two research questions on page 63. Which paragraph of the results section answers each question?

1. Research Question 1: Results Paragraph: ____

2. Research Question 2: Results Paragraph: ____

C. How is each paragraph in the results section organized? Discuss your answer with a small group.

Collaborative Writing

A. In a small group, choose a topic related to the use of technology. Survey people in your class, institution, or community. Use one of these topics or write your own.

- ☐ the use of cell phones (or another technology)
- ☐ attitudes toward technology in teaching and learning
- ☐ preferences for e-books compared with print books
- ☐ the impact of technology on daily life
- ☐ the amount of time spent using technology compared with other activities
- ☐ your idea: _____

B. With your group, write five questions for a survey on the topic you chose in activity A. You can use these questions as models or write your own.

How often do you use your cell phone?

Do you agree with this statement: "I can concentrate on a lecture and text at the same time"?

Strongly Agree – Agree – Neither Agree nor Disagree – Disagree – Strongly Disagree

How much do you think the Internet has improved your life on a scale of 1 (not at all) to 5 (very much)?

Which of these mobile devices do you use regularly?

- ☐ smartphone
- ☐ laptop computer
- ☐ tablet
- ☐ other: _____

1. _____
2. _____
3. _____
4. _____
5. _____

C. In your group, conduct your survey and collect data.

D. Analyze the data you collected. Complete at least three of these sentences using your data.

1. A majority of _____ thought _____.
2. Only _____% of students said _____.
3. Almost all participants reported _____.
4. Approximately half of the _____ believed _____.
5. More _____ than _____ said _____.
6. Almost no students thought _____.

E. Work together to write a results section. Write one or two paragraphs. Use the sentences from activity D to help you. If possible, divide your results into groups and organize them in order of importance or surprise.

F. Compare your results section with another group's. Discuss these questions together.

   a. Do you understand the results of the survey?

   b. Which results are most important or surprising?

   c. What other information would you like to know from this survey?

   d. Are there any sentences or results you don't understand?

Independent Writing

A. You are going to write a research paper about the research you conducted in the Collaborative Writing activity or another survey you choose to do. Answer these questions about your research.

Introduction

1. Why did you do the research? _____

   _____

2. What were your research questions?

   Research Question 1: _____

   Research Question 2: _____

   _____

3. What did you expect to find? _____

   _____

Methods

4. How many people did you survey? _____

5. What do you know about the participants? _____

   _____

6. What questions did you ask? Which research question does each survey question answer?

   _____

   _____

   _____

7. What are the most important data? _____

   _____

8. What are the most surprising data? _____

_____

9. What trends did you observe? Did some groups of participants answer

differently than other groups? _____

_____

Discussion

10. How do the data answer your research questions?

Research Question 1: _____

_____

Research Question 2: _____

_____

Other Research Questions: _____

_____

Results

11. How can you explain your results? What do they mean?

_____

_____

12. What are your conclusions about the topic? _____

_____

B. Look at your data. Choose how you will report your data.

☐ table of numbers   ☐ pie chart

☐ bar chart   ☐ other: _____

☐ line graph

C. Look at the synonyms in the Vocabulary Tip box. Write down the ones you can use in a research paper about your survey. Add at least one more set of synonyms that is relevant to the topic of your research.

D. Write a research paper to report on your survey. Use the four standard subheadings (*Introduction*, *Methods*, *Results*, and *Discussion*). If you use additional sources, include a page of references (see page 64). Use the passive voice to describe your methods and avoid general subjects and personal pronouns. Use target vocabulary from page 61.

VOCABULARY TIP

Use synonyms to avoid repeating key words too frequently. For example:

- *research, study, project, survey, questionnaire*

- *participants, respondents, students, men, women*

- *cell phone, mobile phone, smartphone, mobile device*

A. Read your research paper. Answer the questions below, and make revisions as needed.

1. Check (✓) the information you included in your paper.

☐ reasons you did the research

☐ methods

☐ charts and tables

☐ conclusions

☐ research questions and/or expected findings

☐ highlights of key results

☐ explanations and interpretations

☐ references

2. Look at the information you did not include. Would adding that information make your research paper more complete?

Grammar for Editing Passive Voice and Active Voice

1. Intransitive verbs (verbs that cannot take a direct object) have no passive form.

   Problems ~~were~~ happened in class.

2. Do not confuse the present perfect with the passive voice. Perfect tenses use *have* as the auxiliary verb. Passive verbs use *be*.

   Research has ^*been* conducted into texting in class.

3. If the subject performs the action (that is, if the subject is the agent), the verb must be in the active voice.

   Scientists have ~~been~~ studied the effects of texting in class.

B. Check the language in your research paper. Revise and edit as needed.

Language Checklist
☐ I used target words in my research paper.
☐ I used synonyms effectively.
☐ I used passive voice to avoid general subjects and improve cohesion.
☐ I edited for common errors with passive voice.

C. Check your research paper again. Repeat activities A and B.

Self-Assessment Review: Go back to page 61 and reassess your knowledge of the target vocabulary. How has your understanding of the words changed? What words do you feel most comfortable using now?

UNIT 6

Everyday Economics

In this unit, you will

> analyze explanations and learn how they are used in academic writing.
> use cause and effect in an explanation.
> increase your understanding of the target academic words for this unit.

WRITING SKILLS

> Cause and Effect
> Supporting with Reasons
> **GRAMMAR** Verb + *–ing* Form

Self-Assessment

Think about how well you know each target word, and check (✓) the appropriate column. I have...

TARGET WORDS	never seen this word before.	heard or seen the word but am not sure what it means.	heard or seen the word and understand what it means.	used the word confidently in *either* speaking or writing.
AWL				
🔑 accompany				
🔑 adjust				
coherent				
🔑 definite				
🔑 ensure				
fluctuate				
incline				
🔑 injure				
nonetheless				
🔑 occupy				
perceive				
presume				
prime				
thereby				

🔑 Oxford 3000™ keywords

Building Knowledge

Read these questions. Discuss your answers in a small group.

1. Economics is the study of the way money, business, and industry are organized. Have you ever taken an economics class? Why, or why not?

2. According to the economic principle of supply and demand, prices rise and fall with the availability of an item. How do the prices of apartments change when there are few apartments available?

3. According to the cost-benefit principle, any cost should also have a benefit. What benefit have you received from buying an electronic device?

Writing Model

An explanation essay is a common assignment in university courses. Read the economics course assignment below and the two student response example essays.

Assignment: Explanation Essay

ECON101

Fall semester 2014

Two economic principles that we have studied in the course so far are cost-benefit and supply and demand. As you have learned, choices that consumers and businesses make are influenced by a cost-benefit principle. We will spend money only if we see a valuable benefit from spending it. According to the supply-and-demand principle, when the demand for a product or service increases, the price will also rise. However, if the available supply of the product or service increases, the price will decrease.

For one of your assignments, you will write an essay about a real-world example of an interesting economic situation. The situation should relate to either the cost-benefit or the supply-and-demand principle. Your essay should be 300–500 words, and it should present a clear observation and a coherent explanation. On the following pages are two example essays, adapted from student essays from *The Economic Naturalist* by Robert H. Frank (Basic Books, 2007).

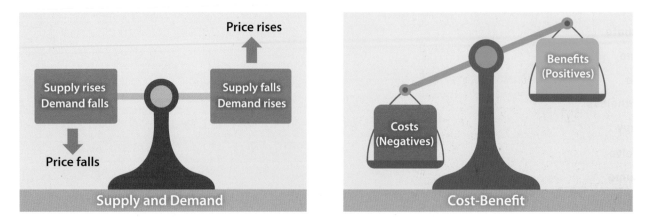

Student Response – Example Essay 1

by Rhonda Hadi

Why are hotel prices in Sharm El Sheikh in Egypt lowest during periods of highest occupancy?

Normally hotel rates **fluctuate** during the year, reflecting the seasonal demand for hotel rooms. When there is a great demand for hotel rooms, the room rates are usually higher. During **prime** times such as vacation or holidays, hotels in some areas will have almost every room **occupied**. Consequently, customers willingly[1] pay the higher room rates. In Sharm El Sheikh, a resort town in Egypt, **occupancy** rates[2] for hotels are much higher during the summer than during the winter. Fewer people visit Sharm El Sheikh during the winter months. Therefore, you would **presume** that the summer room rates would be more expensive because the demand is greater. Why, then, are room rates in Sharm El Sheikh significantly lower in the summer months?

In answering this question, it is clear that hotel room prices depend on more than just high demand. Hotel owners also consider the willingness and ability of potential customers to pay the room rate. Winter guests tend to be Europeans and other high-income Westerners. They choose Sharm El Sheikh because its weather is a relief from cold northern European climates. They are willing and able to pay the higher room rates.

In contrast, tourists from Egypt and elsewhere in the Middle East do not have very cold winters. Therefore, they do not look for warm winter vacation destinations. They prefer to visit a resort like Sharm El Sheikh in the summer, during typical school and work vacations. These visitors are usually families, and they are less **inclined** to pay a high room rate. For this reason, hotel owners cannot charge the highest rates in the summer, even though it is the time of highest **occupancy**. Hotel owners **adjust** their prices based on customers in their markets as well as the **perceived** demand.

---

[1] *willingly:* doing something without objecting
[2] *occupancy rates:* the percentage of rooms that are occupied

Sharm El Sheikh

Student Response – Example Essay 2

by Greg Balet

Why are child safety seats required in cars but not in airplanes?

In the United States, federal law requires that a young child be in a car safety seat,[1] even for a short drive to the grocery store. Yet you can hold a child under two on your lap[2] when you fly from New York to Los Angeles or from Dubai to London. What explains
5 this difference?

Some think this difference is because if the plane crashes, you are going to die anyway, strapped[3] in or not. That may be true, but **nonetheless** there are many other things that can happen during a flight—severe air turbulence,[4] for example. Wearing a seat belt helps to **ensure** the safety of all air passengers, **thereby** resulting in fewer
10 **injuries**.

When you consider the costs and benefits, however, you will find a more believable explanation. Once you have purchased a child safety seat, it costs nothing to strap your child into it every time you take your child in the car. The additional cost is zero. The benefit is improved safety for your child. Therefore, strapping your child in while
15 traveling in your car **definitely** makes sense. If you are on a full flight from New York to Los Angeles, however, you must buy an extra ticket for your child to be in a safety seat. This ticket might cost you $1,000. Because of the high price, many parents do not buy the extra ticket when a young child **accompanies** them on a flight. An airplane accident is many times less likely than a car accident. Parents may not see the benefit of the safety
20 seat when the risk is low.

People may not want to admit that they didn't want to spend money for the safest option on a plane for their child. However, that is essentially what the parents' choice means. So they hold tight to their children and hope for the best, rather than pay $1,000 for an extra seat.

---

[1] *car safety seat:* a special portable safety seat for a child that can be fitted into a car
[2] *lap:* the top part of your legs that forms a flat surface when you are sitting down
[3] *strapped:* fastened using a strap or belt
[4] *air turbulence:* a series of sudden and violent changes in the direction that air is moving in

LEARN

When you explain why something occurs, you can focus on causes and effects.

- Decide if you will focus on the causes, on the effects, or on both. If it is a short essay, the topic may be too broad to cover both causes and effects.

  A **causal analysis** will look at several causes that have resulted in the situation. Use the words and phrases *because, since, as, due to, because of,* and *as a result/consequence*.

  An **effect analysis** will look at one cause (a major event or reason) and will focus on the various effects. Use the words and phrases *so, as as result, for this reason, therefore, consequently, cause, result in,* and *thereby*.

- Support your key points with observations, data, facts, or other evidence.

APPLY

A. Read the statements about student response example essay 1 on page 79. Label the cause (*C*) and effect (*E*). Circle the phrases that signal a cause-and-effect relationship.

1. During the holidays, hotels are fully occupied. Consequently, guests are willing to pay higher room prices.

2. Few Egyptians go to Sharm El Sheikh in the winter because of their country's mild winter weather.

3. Due to cold northern European winters, some Europeans go to Sharm El Sheikh, where it is warmer.

4. Egyptian families often go to Sharm El Sheikh during summer vacations, but they are not willing or able to pay high hotel rates. Therefore, hotel owners cannot charge high rates during the summer.

B. Write cause-and-effect statements. You may combine the sentence pairs into one sentence, or you may have two sentences.

1. Laws do not require young children to wear a seat belt on a plane. Parents may choose to hold them in their laps.

   Laws do not require young children to wear a seat belt on a plane. Therefore,

   parents may choose to hold them in their laps.

2. Most parents always use child safety seats in a car. It is required by law.

   _____

3. Recently, more and more drivers are distracted by their cell phones. Some countries now ban the use of cell phones while driving.

   _____

Analyze

A. For each of the two example essays on pages 79 and 80, number the order in which each item appears.

Example Essay 1	Example Essay 2
___ Contrast European tourists with Egyptian tourists.	___ Explain the situation and restate the question posed before the essay.
_1_ Explain what usually happens worldwide.	___ Summarize, explaining the real cause for the situation.
___ State the thesis, giving an answer to the question posed before the essay.	___ Present an explanation that is not adequate, in the writer's opinion.
___ Restate the question posed before the essay.	___ Present an explanation that explains the reasons for the situation.
___ Give a conclusion based on observations.	
___ Describe the winter hotel guests.	

B. Answer the questions about the writing model on pages 78–80. Then discuss your answers with a partner.

1. Who is the audience for the assignment on page 78?

2. Which example essay is an example of the cost-benefit principle? What is the cost? What is the benefit?

3. Which example essay is an example of the supply-and-demand principle? What is the supply? What is the demand?

4. For each example essay, the writer uses general observations and common knowledge for support. Are general observations and common knowledge adequate support for this assignment? Why, or why not?

C. In a small group, discuss the question below.

Which explanation was more convincing to you, student response example essay 1 or example essay 2? Give specific reasons for your answer.

A. Complete the Word Form Chart. Use a dictionary to check your answers. Compare your answers with a partner.

Word Form Chart			
Noun	**Verb**	**Adjective**	**Adverb**
fluctuation	fluctuate	_____	_____
inclination	incline		_____
occupation	occupy	occupied / unoccupied	_____
perception	perceive	_____	_____
presumption	presume	_____	

B. Use words from the chart to complete the sentences. Change the verb or noun form if necessary.

1. When the economy is strong, the _occupation_ rate in area office buildings is very high. Almost every available office space is rented.

2. When the economy is weak, many office building are _unoccupied_ They are vacant.

3. Since the number of employees ~~incline~~ _fluctuates_ with changes in the economy, in some years there are more employees than in others.

4. When consumers are uncertain about their job security, they are less _inclined_ to spend money on a new car or a house.

5. The article states that the economy has shown signs of improvement. _Presumably_, one of the signs is the lower unemployment rate.

6. In spite of the common _perception_ that older workers cannot be retrained, evidence shows that special training courses are very effective.

7. Some unemployed older workers may decide to get training for a new _occupation_.

The adjective *prime* has several similar meanings. Look at some of the collocations.

1. main or most important

Collocations: *prime* objective, of *prime* importance, *prime* concern; *prime* minister; *prime* times; *prime* suspect

2. best quality; excellent

Collocations: *prime* location; *prime* cut of beef; *prime* real estate

3. most suitable

Collocations: *prime* candidate; *prime* target for crime; *prime* example

CORPUS

C. **Complete the sentences with *prime* plus a collocation.**

1. The new hotel has been successful due to its _prime location_ downtown.

2. Finding a hotel at the right price in the right location is of _prime importance_ for families making vacation plans.

3. Tonight there is a _prime times_ TV documentary about airline safety. It will be shown during the time when there are the most viewers.

4. The _prime minister_ met with her cabinet members and advisors to talk about the cost-benefit analysis of the proposed convention center.

5. After interviewing seven people, the manager called the _prime candidate_ to return for a second interview.

Vocabulary Activities STEP II: Sentence Level

The adjective *definite* means "certain or sure; unlikely to change." The prefix *in-* indicates the negative and means "not." *Indefinite* means "uncertain."

He has **definite** ideas about how to improve the economy.

Her plans for the future are **indefinite**.

The adverb forms are *definitely* and *indefinitely*. The adverb *indefinitely* usually refers to an uncertain amount of time.

You should **definitely** review your notes before the test.

Due to the fire, the store will be closed **indefinitely**.

The adjectives *definite* and *definitive* are often confused. *Definitive* means "final" or "considered to be the best of its kind and almost impossible to improve."

The lawyers reached a **definitive** agreement.

The new book is considered the **definitive** biography of the former president.

CORPUS

D. Answer the questions using the correct form of the word *definite* or *indefinite*. Discuss your answers with a partner.

1. What large purchase are you planning to make in the future?

2. Do you anticipate any future price increases on the goods or services we buy?

3. What goods or services do you anticipate being available and affordable for a long time and probably will remain that way?

Nonetheless is an adverb meaning "despite this fact." It is used in formal contexts. *Nevertheless* is a synonym.

> The problems are serious and complicated. **Nonetheless**, we need to address them immediately.

> We **nevertheless** need to address them immediately.

Thereby is an adverb used to introduce the result of an action or situation already mentioned. It is a formal term, and it is usually followed by the *-ing* form.

> Exercise strengthens the heart, **thereby** reducing the risk of heart attack.

CORPUS

E. Use the prompts. Write sentences that begin with *nonetheless*.

1. We booked our hotel during the peak season.

   Nonetheless, the price was very inexpensive.

2. The hotel was built over 50 years ago.

   Nonetheless, ~~the hotel still~~ new. It feels new. it has flat screen TVs and free Wi-fi.

3. Most travelers are inconvenienced by security lines at the airport.

   Nonetheless, the lines are going fast.

4. Most airlines charge a fee to check a suitcase.

   Nonetheless, the fee is inexpensive.

F. Complete each sentence with a clause about the result. Use *thereby*.

1. The seasoned traveler books airplane flights far in advance, *thereby getting a good price and schedule.*

2. It is best to not carry large sums of money when you travel, thereby saving yourself from attacks or thieves.

3. Credit card companies charge an extra fee for foreign purchases, thereby eaning those companies more money.

G. Answer the questions. Use a form of the word in **bold** in your answer. You can change the word form.

1. What kinds of **injuries** can happen due to air turbulence?

   _____

2. Why is it important for airplane safety information to be **coherent**?

   _____

3. When you were young, who **accompanied** you on your vacations or trips?

   _____

4. What **adjustments** can a person make to travel or vacation plans in order to save money?

   _____

5. What can you do to **ensure** that you have a quiet room at a hotel?

   _____

Grammar   Verb + -*ing* Form

The -*ing* form is common in academic writing and can add variety to your sentences.

1. The -*ing* form is used in reduced non-defining adjective clauses. (See Unit 2, page 25.) These clauses are useful for showing cause and effect. Commonly used forms include *causing, implying, leading to, meaning, reflecting, resulting in, requiring, suggesting,* and *using.*

   Fewer tourists visit in the winter, **_resulting in_** many unoccupied hotel rooms.

2. The -*ing* form can function as a noun and be the subject of a sentence. The -*ing* phrase is always singular.

   Wearing seat belts helps to ensure the safety of all passengers.

3. The -*ing* form follows certain phrases.

   a. Useful verb + preposition + -*ing* form combinations: *complain about, get used to, good at, insist on, look forward to, succeed in*

      The father **_insisted on holding his son_** in his lap.

   b. Useful adjective + preposition + -*ing* form combinations: *adjust to, anxious about, aware of, interested in, responsible for, similar to, skilled at*

      Most parents are **_anxious about traveling with an infant_**.

A. Combine the sentence pairs into a single sentence. Use an -ing clause.

1. New cell phones are introduced every year. ~~This leads~~ _, leading_ customers to buy updated models with more features.

   New cell phones are introduced every year, leading customers to buy updated

   models with more features.

2. Customers eagerly follow news about the latest electronic devices. This reflects the wide appeal of new technology.

   _____

3. Hundreds of new devices are introduced every year. ~~This causes~~ _Causing_ older devices to quickly become outdated.

   _____

4. New products are often incompatible with older software. ~~This requires~~ _requiring_ customers to purchase new software as well.

   _____

5. The market for electronic devices is extremely competitive. ~~This means~~ _meaning_ companies must be constantly offering new and innovative products.

   _____

B. Complete the sentences in your own words. Use an -ing verb from the box. You will use one of them more than once.

causing	leading to	meaning	resulting in

1. Last year, the hotel industry suffered due to bad weather. There was a severe hurricane in August, ___leading to___

2. High winds carried torrential rain, ___causing floods.___

3. The airport was closed for several days, ___meaning there were no flight.___

4. Since there is usually no cancellation fee on a hotel room, most people simply canceled their reservations, ___resulting in lost money.___

5. A month later, many hotels are still closed for repair work, ___leading to___
   ___more lost money.___

C. Rewrite each sentence. Begin with the -*ing* form of the underlined word as the subject. You will need to reword other parts of the sentence, too.

1. International <u>travel</u> can be very tiring, so hotel managers should make rooms comfortable and relaxing.

   Traveling internationally can be very tiring, so hotel managers should make rooms

   comfortable and relaxing.

2. <u>Adjustment</u> to a time change and jet lag can take a traveler several days.

   _____

   _____

3. It's important to <u>ensure</u> that hotel guests can rest quietly at any time of day.

   _____

   _____

4. It's a good business practice to be <u>sensitive</u> to the needs of international travelers.

   _____

   _____

D. Complete each sentence in your own words. Use the correct preposition and an -*ing* form.

1. Because of my injury, I complained *about having to do chores around the house* .

2. I am inclined to be anxious _____.

3. This year, I have had to get used _____.

4. After I graduate, I look forward _____.

5. I hope to succeed _____.

6. I would like to be skilled _____.

7. I would like a job in which I am responsible _____.

WRITING SKILL — Supporting with Reasons

LEARN

When writing an explanation, you want to convince the reader that your thesis is sound and that your arguments are logical. You want the reader to agree with your thesis. One way to support your thesis is with reasons, which answer the question "Why?" To be convincing, keep these points in mind:

- Is your reason based on common knowledge? Can you assume that your reader shares the same knowledge and will agree with you?

- Make sure that the reason is logical. Does the reason support your argument in most situations?

- Consider the order of your reasons. Which reason will you start with? Will you organize the reasons in sequential order? In order of importance? From minor points to major points? There is no one correct order. Use the order that works best for your argument.

- Does one reason lead to the next reason? Are your reasons related to one another in the order in which they are presented?

APPLY

A. For each question below, list three reasons to explain the observation.

1. In many parts of the world, newspaper sales have decreased. This is partly due to people reading the news on the Internet. Why do many newspapers offer free news online but charge for a printed newspaper?

   a. *Newspapers don't have a good way to charge for reading stories online.*

   b. _____

   c. _____

2. When a company releases a new electronic device with many completely new features, the price is usually very high. Later versions are usually less expensive. Why do customers pay the high price for new technology when prices for similar products will be lower within a year?

   a. _____

   b. _____

   c. _____

B. Compare your reasons in activity A with a partner. Choose the strongest three reasons between both of your answers. In what order would you present them in a written explanation? Number them.

Collaborative Writing

A. Read the student notes about an economics assignment. Which reasons do you think are the strongest? Circle the letters.

> *Why is the taxi fare from JFK Airport in New York to any part of Manhattan a flat rate of $52.00 plus tolls? Why isn't it a metered rate, based on miles traveled? Metered rates are used for all other taxi fares in New York.*
>
> *a. Many travelers don't have much money to spend. Maybe travelers don't carry cash. A flat rate is less expensive for travelers.*
> *b. Many travelers in New York don't speak English. Some taxi drivers could take advantage of them by charging a higher rate.*
> *c. New York is a popular tourist destination, so the city wants to make a good first impression. The city doesn't want travelers to feel taken advantage of by dishonest taxi drivers.*
> *d. Some drivers might take a longer route to increase the fare.*
> *e. Many visitors don't know their way around the city.*
> *f. The city wants to encourage people to take taxis from the airport.*

B. Compare your answers for activity A with a partner. Answer the questions.

1. What is another reason you could use in an explanation paragraph?

2. What order would you put your reasons in?

C. With your partner, write an explanation paragraph, using reasons. Make sure that your reasons are clear and in a logical sequence. As in the student response example essays on pages 79–80, state the question first. For example, you can start your paragraph like this:

> *Why is the taxi fare from JFK Airport in New York to any part of Manhattan a flat rate of $52.00 plus tolls? Why isn't it a metered rate, based on miles traveled?*
>
> *Although taxis use a metered rate throughout New York City, they use a flat rate from JFK Airport to any part of Manhattan. Why is this?*

D. Conclude your paragraph with a sentence that supports or restates your thesis.

> *It seems that keeping tourists happy is the main reason for this flat rate.*

E. Compare your paragraph with another pair's. Discuss these questions.

1. Did you use similar reasons? Which reasons were different?

2. Was the order of your reasons different? Which order was more effective?

3. What changes can you make to your paragraph to improve it?

Independent Writing

A. You are going to write an explanation essay. First, consider these questions about economic observations. Take notes about causes, effects, and reasons.

1. In some areas, newspapers are sold in vending machines where the buyer opens a door and takes a paper. The machine is simple but allows the buyer to take more papers than paid for. Why do companies use this type of vending machine for newspapers? Most machines (such as those selling drinks) allow a buyer to receive only one item. These vending machines are complex and expensive.

2. In some countries, why is milk sold in rectangular containers while soft drinks are sold in round containers?

3. When a country hosts the Olympic Games, it spends millions of dollars on preparation, including new buildings and accommodations. The cost seems to be greater than the financial gains. In spite of this, how do the Olympics benefit a country? Are any of those benefits financial?

B. Choose one of the questions in activity A as a topic for an explanation essay. Consider the ideas in the chart to plan your writing.

Economic observation question
1. Explanation of the situation, including background information
2. Thesis (You may also include a restatement of the question.)
3. Clear presentation of the reasons to support your thesis, including causes
4. Conclusion with restatement of the thesis

C. Write several causal statements for your essay, using the words and phrases in parentheses.

1. (because) _____

2. (as a result) _____

3. (causing) _____

4. (leading to) _____

D. Look at the phrases in the Vocabulary Tip box. Write three sentences that you can use in your explanation.

1. _____

2. _____

3. _____

> **VOCABULARY TIP**
>
> These terms are useful when writing about changes that influence economic decisions.
>
> This *has an effect on / influences / contributes to* ...
>
> This *has a positive / negative impact on* ...
>
> It can *enhance / transform / develop* ...

E. Write your explanation essay, using your planning notes and sentences from activities C and D. Include reasons, causes, and effects in your explanation. Use target vocabulary from page 77.

REVISE AND EDIT

A. Read your essay. Answer the questions below, and make revisions as needed.

1. Check (✓) the information you included in your essay.

   ☐ economic observation question
   ☐ explanation of the situation
   ☐ clear thesis statement
   ☐ causal statements

   ☐ several points, logically supported with reasons
   ☐ conclusion with restatement of the thesis

2. Look at the information you did not include. Would adding that information make your essay more complete?

Grammar for Editing | Commas

1. Use commas to set off non-defining adjective clauses.

   My economic class, which meets only once a week, is very challenging.

   My professor assumed that I had an accounting background, which was not true.

2. Use commas to set off *-ing* clauses.

   The project didn't have an agreed-upon schedule, leading to misunderstandings.

3. Use commas to set off adverbial clauses at the beginning of a sentence.

   After they adjusted the machine, it continued to break down often.

Exceptions: *Although, even though, though, while,* and *whereas* usually require a comma when they are used after the main clause.

   The machine continued to break down, even though they had adjusted it.

4. Use commas to set off transitional words.

   Nonetheless, they would not purchase a new machine.

B. Check the language in your essay. Revise and edit as needed.

Language Checklist
☐ I used target words in my explanation essay.
☐ I used appropriate terms to write about economics.
☐ I used *-ing* forms correctly.
☐ I edited for common errors with commas.

C. Check your research paper again. Repeat activities A and B.

Self-Assessment Review: Go back to page 77 and reassess your
knowledge of the target vocabulary. How has your understanding of the words
changed? What words do you feel most comfortable using now?

UNIT 7

Borrowing or Stealing?

In this unit, you will

> analyze discussion board posts and learn how they are used in academic classes.
> use argumentative writing to challenge a position.
> increase your understanding of the target academic words for this unit.

WRITING SKILLS

> Using Sources
> Quotations
> **GRAMMAR** Noun Clauses

Self-Assessment

Think about how well you know each target word, and check (✓) the appropriate column. I have...

TARGET WORDS	never seen this word before.	heard or seen the word but am not sure what it means.	heard or seen the word and understand what it means.	used the word confidently in *either* speaking or writing.
AWL				
ambiguous				
arbitrary				
cite				
consequent				
deviate				
distort				
domain				
enforce				
explicit				
exploit				
implement				
inspect				
integrate				
orient				

Building Knowledge

Read these questions. Discuss your answers in a small group.

1. Does your school or university have a plagiarism or academic honesty policy? What is it?

2. Is it acceptable for novelists to use sentences from other novels in their books?

3. Have you participated in an online discussion? What happened?

Writing Models

A discussion board is a website that allows teachers and students to participate in an online discussion or submit assignments online. Read a professor's question and a student's essay answer.

Is Plagiarism Always Dishonest?

POSTED BY PROFESSOR SANFORD ON TUESDAY AT 3:30 P.M.

Before you start your major writing assignments for English 101, you need to think about the issue of plagiarism. As you learned during new student **orientation**, plagiarism is commonly defined as

5 taking another person's words or ideas and using them in your own work without correct acknowledgement (for example, quotation and/or **citation**). Explain in a multi-paragraph essay why you agree or disagree with this statement: "Plagiarism is clearly an act of dishonesty; it is never **ambiguous**."

___ NEWEST ▼   WRITE A COMMENT

POSTED THURSDAY AT 9:12 P.M.
Hilary Painter

10 There is no doubt that some acts of plagiarism are deliberate attempts to deceive[1] teachers and cheat in class.

___
[1]*deceive:* try to make someone believe something that is not true

For example, if I copied an essay or even a paragraph from a website and turned it in as part of an assignment, it would be plagiarism. I would face severe **consequences** such as a failing grade for the paper or even the whole course. The same is true for submitting another student's paper, **distorting** the work of another writer, or copying from a classmate on a test. The academic dishonesty rules would be strictly **enforced**. However, there is a substantial gray area[2] between acceptable and unacceptable use of sources. Therefore, I believe that there is actually **ambiguity** in some cases of plagiarism.

A recent example highlights this difficulty. A young German writer was accused of copying passages from other novels in her most recent book. Her defense was that as a novelist, she was creatively **integrating**, or "mixing," other works of literature into her writing (Gardner, 2010). **Consequently**, she argued that her novel was no different from the plays of William Shakespeare. Shakespeare famously borrowed stories and even direct quotations from historical sources. There are examples of this in other **domains** in today's culture, too. Modern musicians regularly "remix" tunes and words from other songs into original new tracks (Gardner, 2010). These musicians claim that all ideas have already been expressed. Therefore, the work of the artist is to reuse them in a meaningful way. In this case, though, critics are split on the author's use of other novels. If she has created something new and original out of her sources, then the book is an artistic remix. If she has simply cut-and-pasted, then it is plagiarism.

Compared to novelists, students have clearer rules for avoiding plagiarism. Therefore, it might be argued that plagiarism is **unambiguous** in academia. However, this would not be true. Even university professors are sometimes accused of academic dishonesty. For instance, a group of malaria[3] researchers led by Paula Breitlinger of the University of Washington, Seattle, closely **inspected** a literature review[4] written by two Nigerian professors (Uneke & Ogbonna, 2009). They found at least 3,000 words of "unattributed[5] quotations and close paraphrases" (Breitlinger et al., 2009, p. 855). Uneke and Ogbonna

---

[2]*gray area:* an area of a subject or situation that is not clear
[3]*malaria:* a serious disease in hot countries that you get from the bite of a mosquito
[4]*literature review:* a summary of information or research on a particular topic
[5]*unattributed:* without saying that someone else is responsible for doing, saying, or writing something

responded in the same issue of the journal that they had provided **explicit** references to every source. Furthermore, because their article was a literature review, not original research, they contended that similarities with the sources were unavoidable. Finally, they argued that it is acceptable to use exact sentences in order not "to introduce errors in the process" (Uneke & Ogbonna, 2009, p. 856) and **deviate** from the original authors' meaning. The editors of the journal ultimately published the review, Breitlinger et al.'s letter, and the authors' response. Therefore, it might be asked whether Uneke and Ogbonna suffered any **consequences** from this incident. While they did see their paper published, their names will always be linked to accusations of plagiarism. They might find it more difficult to publish in academic journals in the future.

In conclusion, I do not believe schools can **implement** a simple plagiarism policy. Instead, it is important to see each case in its own context. Many cases of student plagiarism are clear: The student intentionally **exploited** information found on the Internet or turned in a friend's paper to avoid doing the work. However, sometimes there is a gray area. The student might try to write honestly but not understand the rules of **citation**, paraphrasing, and quotation. In my opinion, the professor should provide instruction, not punishment. In rare cases, it might not be obvious whether or not information can be used without **citation**. This was seen in both the examples I introduced. A conversation between the teacher and student should resolve this confusion since professors understand how **citation** works in their particular **domain**. This will help them to make decisions about student writing that are not **arbitrary** but rather based on actual use of sources. In this way, cases of possible plagiarism can be seen as a learning opportunity, not as an **unambiguous deviation**.

References

Breitlinger, P. E., Behrens, C. B., Micek, M. A., Steketee, R. W., Andrews, K. T., Skinner-Adams, T. S., … Ayisi, J. (2009). Correspondence: Plagiarism. *Transactions of the Royal Society of Tropical Medicine and Hygiene, 103*, 855.

Gardner, T. (2010, February 17). Mixing or plagiarizing? *NCTE Inbox Blog*. Retrieved from http://ncteinbox.blogspot.com/ 2010/02/mixing-or-plagiarizing.html

Uneke, C. J., & Ogbonna A. (2009). Malaria and HIV co-infection in pregnancy in sub-Saharan Africa: Impact of treatment using antimalarial and antiretroviral agents. *Transactions of the Royal Society of Tropical Medicine and Hygiene, 103*, 761–767.

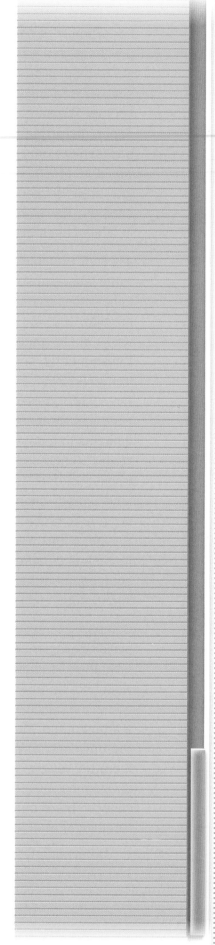

LEARN

Academic writers need to tell readers where they found all of their information. Providing source information is important not only to avoid plagiarism, but also to strengthen your writing. It shows that you have researched your topic thoroughly. You can also show which experts support your ideas and which authorities have different opinions. When you use sources to write an assignment, follow these steps:

1. Keep accurate notes on your reading so that you remember where you found each idea.

2. Put exact words from the sources in quotation marks.

3. Paraphrase and summarize your sources in your own words wherever possible (see page 26).

4. Write the correct citation in parentheses after every quotation, summary, and paraphrase.

5. At the end of your assignment, start a new page with the heading *References* and write complete references for your sources.

There are several different formats for citations and references. The writing model on page 96 uses the American Psychological Association (APA) style. In APA style, citations are written in parentheses with the author's last name, the year of publication, and—for quotations only—the page number. References include all the information the reader needs to find the source in print or online.

APPLY

A. Identify the parts of the citations using the labels from the box. You will not use every label in both citations.

first author	page number	other authors	year of publication

a. _____ b. _____
1. (Gardner, 2010)

a. _____ b. _____ c. _____ d. _____
2. (Breitlinger et al., 2009, p. 855)

B. Identify the parts of the references. Use the labels from the box. You will not use every label in both references.

author's family name	journal name	volume number
author's initial	page numbers	website address
article title	publication date	website name

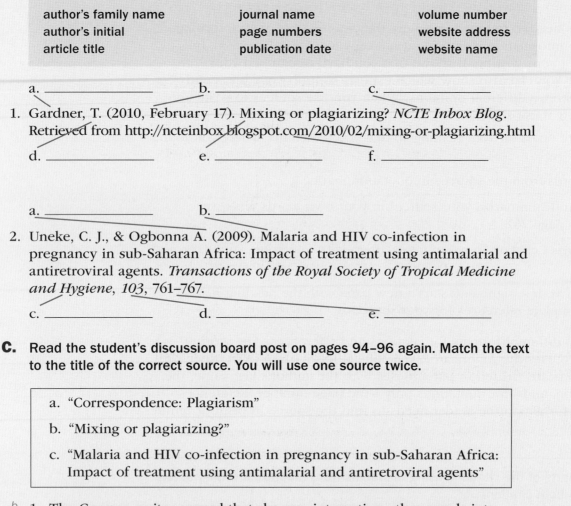

a. _____   b. _____   c. _____

1. Gardner, T. (2010, February 17). Mixing or plagiarizing? *NCTE Inbox Blog.*
   Retrieved from http://ncteinbox.blogspot.com/2010/02/mixing-or-plagiarizing.html

d. _____   e. _____   f. _____

a. _____   b. _____

2. Uneke, C. J., & Ogbonna A. (2009). Malaria and HIV co-infection in
   pregnancy in sub-Saharan Africa: Impact of treatment using antimalarial and
   antiretroviral agents. *Transactions of the Royal Society of Tropical Medicine
   and Hygiene, 103,* 761–767.

c. _____   d. _____   e. _____

C. Read the student's discussion board post on pages 94–96 again. Match the text to the title of the correct source. You will use one source twice.

> a. "Correspondence: Plagiarism"
>
> b. "Mixing or plagiarizing?"
>
> c. "Malaria and HIV co-infection in pregnancy in sub-Saharan Africa:
>   Impact of treatment using antimalarial and antiretroviral agents"

_b_ 1. The German writer argued that she was integrating other novels into
     her book.

____ 2. "unattributed quotations and close paraphrases"

____ 3. a literature review written by two Nigerian professors

____ 4. It is acceptable to use exact sentences in order not "to introduce errors
     in the process."

____ 5. Musicians regularly "remix" other songs.

Analyze

A. Choose the best answer for each question about the writing model on
   pages 94–96.

1. Which of the following sentences best expresses the student's opinion?

   a. Plagiarism is always a deliberate attempt to deceive teachers.

   b. Plagiarism is never a clear act of dishonesty.

   c. Some cases of plagiarism are not clearly dishonest.

2. What is the purpose of the first paragraph of the essay?

   a. to list the main ideas in the rest of the essay

   b. to discuss and reject the opinion presented in the professor's post

   c. to give examples of the consequences of plagiarism

3. What is the relationship between the two body paragraphs?

   a. They both analyze examples showing the difficulty of defining plagiarism in different fields.

   b. They give arguments for and against the statement in the professor's post.

   c. They compare differences between the standards of plagiarism in novels and academic writing.

4. What is the purpose of the last paragraph of the student's essay?

   a. to summarize the ideas in the first three paragraphs and leave the reader with a final thought

   b. to consider alternative arguments to the ones presented in the first three paragraphs

   c. to give recommendations based on the argument presented in the first three paragraphs

B. Underline the words and sentences in the writing model that helped you answer the questions in activity A. Discuss your answers with a partner.

Vocabulary Activities STEP I: Word Level

Word Form Chart		
Noun	**Adjective**	**Adverb**
consequence	consequent	consequently
arbitrariness	arbitrary	arbitrarily
_____	explicit	explicitly

A. Complete the sentences with the correct form of a word in the chart.

1. The library _____ canceled my card.

2. The teacher was clear: He _____ said not to use websites as sources.

3. A newspaper reporter was caught copying paragraphs from other articles. _____, he was fired.

4. A negative _____ of plagiarism could be failing a course.

5. Some websites do not give readers a(n) _____ warning that they have a commercial purpose.

The verb *orient* has two meanings:

*1. APA style is **oriented to** / **oriented** toward writers in the social sciences.*
        aimed at, directed toward

*The website is commercially **oriented.***
        has a commercial goal

*2. International students may find it hard to **orient** themselves in a new educational culture.*
        become comfortable

A related verb is *disorient*, meaning "to make someone feel uncomfortable or confused."

*The novel **disorients** readers by changing rapidly between different time periods.*

The corresponding adjective is *disorienting*.

*The transition from high school to college can be **disorienting** for many students.*

CORPUS

B. Replace the underlined words with a form of *orient* or *disorient* and, if necessary, the correct preposition.

1. It is <u>confusing</u> to change time zones.   <u>*disorienting*</u>

2. New employees need time to <u>adapt</u> themselves to their new workplaces.

    _____

3. The journal is <u>targeted at</u> undergraduate students. _____

4. The number of citations in this paragraph <u>confused</u> me. _____

C. Choose the correct ending for each sentence.

<u> c </u> 1. After each paraphrase, write an in-text

_____ 2. The writer deviates

_____ 3. References to Shakespeare are cleverly integrated

_____ 4. There is some ambiguity

_____ 5. Academic honesty policies will be

_____ 6. Peer review is an essential part of the publication process in the scientific

a. from other detective stories by making the main character a criminal.

b. into the movie.

c. citation with the author and date of publication.

d. enforced by an elected panel of students.

e. in the definition of self-plagiarism.

f. domain.

Vocabulary Activities STEP II: Sentence Level

The verb *exploit* and its related noun, *exploitation*, often have a negative meaning, although in some contexts they may be less disapproving.

1. If you *exploit* someone or something, you try to get an advantage for yourself, often at someone else's expense.

   *Companies may **exploit** undocumented workers because they are powerless.*

2. If you *exploit* a situation, you try to make the best of it for yourself. There is not usually a negative meaning here.

   *Schools should be designed to **exploit** every student's potential.*

3. Businesses and scientists can *exploit* something to make a new product or further their research. This is also a positive meaning.

   *These bacteria can be **exploited** to develop new medications.*

4. When referring to natural resources, *exploitation* usually involves getting use or value from them. However, this can have a negative effect on the environment.

   *The **exploitation** of the rainforests for wood has caused irreversible damage.*

CORPUS

D. Answer the questions. Use a form of *exploit* or *exploitation*. Does your sentence have a positive or negative meaning? Circle the correct description. Discuss your answers with a partner.

1. What resources can you take advantage of at your school, college, or university?

   (Positive)/ Negative: _Students can exploit the exercise equipment in the new_

   sports center.

2. How have people damaged the environment in your country or region?

   Positive / Negative: _____

3. How can teachers use technology effectively in the classroom?

   Positive / Negative: _____

4. Some people say that fast-food restaurants take advantage of their employees by offering low wages. Do you agree?

   Positive / Negative: _____

5. How can solar or wind power be used?

   Positive / Negative: _____

E. Read this press release. Answer the questions following it. Use the correct form of the target words in parentheses.

Silver Lake Books has asked booksellers to remove from their shelves Jon Tang's book *In My Life*. Following recent newspaper reports, an internal investigation confirmed that Tang's book is not an accurate autobiography. In the book, Tang describes several events that did not, in fact, happen or happened very differently. For example, he says that he lived in five different countries as a child, whereas he only lived in two. It is also not clear at this time whether or not his description of surviving the earthquake in Haiti is true. However, the book has received very positive reviews, so we have decided to re-release it with the words "a novel" clearly printed on the cover. We will also begin checking new books more carefully to ensure they are factual. We regret any inconvenience to our customers. Jon Tang's *In My Life: A Novel* will be available in November.

1. What did Tang do in his book? (distort)

   _____

2. Is Tang's description of the earthquake in Haiti true? (ambiguous)

   _____

3. How did the publisher confirm the newspaper reports? (inspect)

   _____

4. What changes is Silver Lakes Books making to its publishing process? (implement)

   _____

5. Do you think Tang will suffer any negative effects from this situation? (consequence)

   _____

F. Match the collocations from the box with the correct paraphrase. Then write a sentence with each collocation.

| arbitrary decision | enforce a policy | public domain |
| closely inspect | explicit instruction | suffer the consequences |

1. _____explicit instruction_____ direct teaching

   Most English learners benefit from explicit instruction in grammar.

2. _____ look at carefully

   _____

3. _____ free for everyone to use

_____

4. _____ make people follow a rule

_____

5. _____ experience the negative effects

_____

6. _____ choice not based on reason

_____

Grammar | Noun Clauses

A noun clause is a dependent clause that is most often used as the object of a reporting verb (*show, explain, say, claim, argue, suggest*, etc.) or the complement of an adjective (*possible, likely, clear, surprising*, etc.). There are three types of noun clauses:

1. Statements:

noun clause

She argued *that* her novel was no different from the plays of William Shakespeare.

2. *Wh-* word questions:

noun clause

Explain *why* you agree or disagree with this statement.

3. *Yes/no* questions:

noun clause

It might not be obvious *if/whether* this information can be used without citation.

Noun clauses can also be used as noun complements.

noun clause

I do not agree with *the claim* that there is never any ambiguity in cases of plagiarism.

noun clause

The fact that plagiarism is ambiguous means that disagreements will exist.

Be careful to avoid common errors with noun clauses:

1. Do not put a comma after the reporting verb.

She argued, that her novel was no different from the plays of William Shakespeare.

2. Use statement word order.

Explain why do you agree or disagree with this statement.

3. Use correct punctuation.

It might not be obvious whether this information can be used without citation?

4. Do not use two subordinators.

Students often ask that how they can paraphrase better.

A. Read the sentences. Write new sentences that contain them as noun clauses.

1. Definitions of plagiarism vary across cultures.

   It is known _that definitions of plagiarism vary across cultures_____.

2. Is it necessary to cite general knowledge?

   Students often wonder _____.

3. Why do different citations styles exist?

   There are several reasons _____.

4. Novelists often use themes and ideas from other stories.

   Most readers understand _____.

5. How many words can you use from a source?

   Even experts cannot say _____.

6. Why do some professional writers fail to cite their sources?

   It is hard to understand _____.

B. Read the paragraph. Correct five errors in the use and punctuation of noun clauses.

Many students do not know ~~that~~ how to conduct research for a paper. A source is available online does not mean it is appropriate. Therefore, it is always important to ask that the source is reliable. If you do not know who did write the article, it may not be a good source for your paper. Some teachers state, that only peer-reviewed articles are acceptable. This means that the source has been checked by two or more experts. These experts tell the editors of the journal whether they should publish the article? Consequently, you can be more confident that the information is accurate.

C. Answer the questions with sentences that use noun clauses.

1. What was the best advice a teacher has given you?

   _Ms. Sharma said that I should learn seven new words a day._____

2. What topics in your major (or any academic discipline) are you interested in?

   _____

3. What is it important for academic writers to do?

   _____

4. What do you understand about plagiarism?

   _____

WRITING SKILL | Using Quotations

LEARN

Sometimes, it is useful to include quotations from your sources. A quotation must be the exact words from the original source. Writers use quotations if they find a phrase that is so unusual, well-written, or important that it is better to use it than paraphrase it. Sometimes, just one or two words are quoted to show that they are unusual, technical, or specific to a source. However, do not use too many quotations in your writing. You must balance your sources' voices with your own. When you use a quotation, follow these steps:

- Decide how much to quote—from a single word to several sentences.

- Copy the words exactly and put them in quotation marks.

- If you make the quotation part of your sentence, make sure it is grammatically correct (e.g., modern musicians regularly "remix" tunes).

- Use square brackets to add or change words or letters (e.g., paraphrasing means "chang[ing] the content"). Use ellipses (…) to omit words.

- Write the citation after the quotation; include a page number if available.

APPLY

Look at the quotations in the writing model on pages 94–96. Why was each one used? Was it very well-written, unusual, very important, or was it allowing the source's author to speak? Discuss your answers with a partner.

Collaborative Writing

A. Read a student's response to another case of possible plagiarism.

> A recent biography of the German philosopher Friedrich Nietzsche (Young, 2010) raises important questions about the ambiguity of quoting sources in academic writing. According to Mark Anderson, a professor at Belmont University, Young's biography includes many sentences that are very similar to another, older book about Nietzsche (Cate, 2005). Young and his supporters have defended his book, arguing that writers are allowed to include historical facts as long as they do not distort the truth and all sources are cited. However, this position is not acceptable. Biography is a serious and difficult genre of writing, and authors of high-quality biographies deserve the same respect as any other writer. While Young's interpretation of Nietzsche was original, his attitude toward biography writing is unprofessional.

B. Check the quotations that would be helpful to add to the paragraph in activity A. Quotations 1 and 2 are from www.plagiarism.org. Quotations 3 and 4 are from Young's response to Anderson in the *Journal of Nietzsche Studies*.

☐ 1. "A paraphrase is a restatement in your own words of someone else's ideas." ("Preventing plagiarism," 2013)

☐ 2. Plagiarism includes "copying words or ideas from someone else without giving credit" ("What is plagiarism?," 2013)

☐ 3. "What are reproduced in my work are occasional phrases of Cate's, never a complete sentence." (Young, 2012, p. 361)

☐ 4. "Since Cate appeared in my bibliography, I assumed it would be obvious that I had used him as a source of basic historical data." (Young, 2012, pp. 361–362)

C. With a partner, rewrite the paragraph in activity A by integrating some quotations from activity B. Remember that you can use a word or phrase from a quotation in your own paragraph as long as you use quotation marks. Change as many sentences as needed, and add the correct citations.

D. Compare your revised paragraph with another pair's. Discuss these questions.

1. Did you choose the same quotations? Why did you choose them?

2. Are there enough quotations or too many quotations?

3. Are all the quotations cited correctly?

Independent Writing

A. You are going to write a challenge to a viewpoint about plagiarism. Many schools have strict policies on plagiarism. Read the definition of *plagiarism* and answer the questions. Discuss them with a small group.

"deliberate [...] representation of another's words, thoughts, or ideas as one's own without attribution in connection with submission of academic work, whether graded or otherwise."

1. Do you think all plagiarism is deliberate? Is any plagiarism accidental?

_____

2. Do you think the same standards of plagiarism should apply to both graded and ungraded work (e.g., informal assignments, proposals, etc.)?

_____

3. At some schools, cases of possible plagiarism are judged by a carefully selected group of students. Is this a good system? Why, or why not?

_____

4. The punishment for the first case of plagiarism at some schools is a failing grade for the course and a one-semester suspension. Why is this fair or unfair?

_____

B. Check (✓) one statement that you strongly disagree with. Then complete the chart.

☐ 1. Schools should severely punish all forms of plagiarism in any assignment on the first offense.

☐ 2. Some plagiarism is accidental and should not be punished.

☐ 3. Only teachers can decide whether a paper is plagiarized and what the appropriate punishment should be.

☐ 4. In order to prevent plagiarism, all major writing assignments should be completed in class and not taken home.

Why do some other people support the statement?	
Why do you disagree with the statement?	
What examples or cases support your opinion?	

C. Collect ideas to support your writing.

1. Find at least two sources. Your sources can be newspaper articles, university websites, journals, or interviews. Write down the references and citations.

   Source 1: Reference: _____

   Citation: (_____)

   Source 2: Reference: _____

   Citation: (_____)

2. Paraphrase the most important and useful ideas in your sources. Write the correct citations.

3. Choose 2–4 good quotations from your sources. Use the correct citations with page numbers if available.

D. Look at the phrases in the Vocabulary Tip box. Write sentences using these phrases that could be helpful for your challenge.

E. Write a challenge to the statement you disagreed with in activity B. Summarize why some people are in favor of the statement. Then explain why you disagree, using phrases from the Vocabulary Tip. Give specific reasons and examples. Make sure you quote and paraphrase your sources correctly. Use target vocabulary from page 93.

> **VOCABULARY TIP**
>
> To disagree politely with a person or idea, use phrases such as the following:
>
> *This opinion is misguided / mistaken / problematic because …*
>
> *I respectfully disagree with Young (2012) since …*
>
> *Young's (2012) argument is invalid / flawed / weak because …*
>
> *Although it is true that …, more importantly …*
>
> *It is also important to note that …*
>
> *An alternative interpretation is …*

REVISE AND EDIT

A. Read your challenge. Answer the questions below, and make revisions as needed.

1. Check (✓) the information you included in your challenge.

   ☐ summary of the argument in favor

   ☐ examples or cases

   ☐ quotations

   ☐ references

   ☐ specific reasons for disagreeing

   ☐ paraphrases

   ☐ citations

2. Look at the information you did not include. Would adding that information make your challenge more interesting to readers?

Grammar for Editing Punctuating Quotations and Citations

Use double quotes (" ") for all quotations. Include commas, periods, question marks, and exclamation points inside the quotation marks.

> She was creatively integrating, or "mixing," other works of literature into her books.

Capitalize the first word of a quotation only in direct quoted speech, not in a noun clause.

> *direct speech*
> The professor said, "The essay is clearly plagiarized."

> *noun clause*
> The professor said that the paper was "clearly plagiarized."

Put a space before a parenthesis, and put punctuation after the citation.

> Modern musicians regularly "remix" tunes and words from other songs into original
> *space* *no space*
> new tracks (Gardner, 2010).

B. Check the language in your challenge. Revise and edit as needed.

Language Checklist
☐ I used target words in my challenge.
☐ I used polite phrases to disagree.
☐ I used noun clauses.
☐ I punctuated quotations and citations correctly.

C. Check your challenge again. Repeat activities A and B.

Self-Assessment Review: Go back to page 93 and reassess your knowledge of the target vocabulary. How has your understanding of the words changed? What words do you feel most comfortable using now?

UNIT 8

A Business Case Analysis

In this unit, you will

> analyze a case analysis essay and learn how it is used in business.
> use problem-solution writing.
> increase your understanding of the target academic words for this unit.

WRITING SKILLS

> Problem and Solution
> Evaluation
> **GRAMMAR** Modals and Adverbs for Hedging

Self-Assessment

Think about how well you know each target word, and check (✓) the appropriate column. I have…

TARGET WORDS	never seen this word before.	heard or seen the word but am not sure what it means.	heard or seen the word and understand what it means.	used the word confidently in *either* speaking or writing.
AWL				
compensate				
convene				
dispose				
🔑 dominate				
erode				
🔑 expose				
immigrate				
🔑 index				
negate				
protocol				
🔑 retain				
scheme				
terminate				
whereby				

🔑 Oxford 3000™ keywords

Building Knowledge

Read these questions. Discuss your answers in a small group.

1. If you were to start a business, what kind of business would it be?

2. What are some of the challenges that you might face in this business?

3. Give an example of a real company or business that faces one of those challenges. How might the company solve the problem?

Writing Model

In a case study essay, also called a case analysis, students write about an actual business and a problem it is facing. Read the essay posted on a website.

Case Analysis of Burger Corner

Burger Corner is a medium-sized, independently owned restaurant in the downtown area of a major city. It is located about five blocks from a state university campus and close to the city's **convention** center. With this prime
5 location, the restaurant has great **exposure** to pedestrians and commuters. It's popular with college students because of the location and reasonable prices. **Convention** attendees often come for dinner. Established about 20 years ago, Burger Corner is known for its hamburgers, hot sandwiches,
10 salads, and homemade desserts. Owners Miguel and Ana García, **immigrants** from Mexico, bought the business about five years ago. Initially, business income seemed to be consistent, but it was not increasing. In the last two years, however, sales have decreased by 20 percent. Recently, the owners have stopped paying themselves
15 any salary. With no **compensation**, they are living off their savings. They realize that unless they make some drastic changes in the next six months, they will certainly be in danger of having to close the business.

Burger Corner is facing the same challenges that many business
20 owners are facing: a poor economy and increasing competition. For the Garcías, these problems have seriously **eroded** profits. However, the stock market **index** has recently shown signs that the

economy is recovering. If the owners can act quickly, they should be able to save their business from failure. However, they must
25 correctly identify the most serious problems and then address them with practical solutions.

On the surface, the main problem seems to be fewer customers. However, it is important to examine the underlying reasons for this problem in order to come up with good solutions. The owners
30 believe that one reason for the decline in customers is a new supermarket in the neighborhood. It features a large selection of ready-to-eat sandwiches, hot meals, and a salad bar. In addition, it has an attractive food court area, which is popular with students. The new supermarket has clearly **eroded** Burger Corner's market
35 share[1] of lunchtime customers.

A recent discovery reveals the second reason for declining business. Last month, the owners found several **negative** online reviews of Burger Corner. They were very surprised, as they do not regularly check online reviews. This is a serious problem. **Negative** online
40 reviews greatly influence customers, especially college students who turn to the Internet for their information. Several reviews cited problems such as poorly trained waitstaff,[3] slow service at lunchtime, and a "tired, outdated décor.[2]" In some ways, these complaints can be a gift to owners: They tell owners what they need
45 to improve. The reviews give the Garcías some insight into what customers perceive as the **negatives** about the restaurant.

When considering solutions, the owners should first identify what already works well for the business. The owners should not make drastic changes that are unnecessary. Burger Corner is already a
50 well-established destination for college students. It has a comfortable, casual feeling, with home-style food served by a young waitstaff. It appeals to young adults and customers who want a unique restaurant. The Garcías fear that the supermarket is taking the lunch crowd from them. This large business may in fact
55 **dominate** the lunchtime market, but the Garcías should not attempt to compete directly with its prices and menus. Rather, they should do more to make Burger Corner stand out and strengthen what is special about it. For example, Burger Corner is comfortable and personal. The supermarket, in contrast, is busy and
60 impersonal; customers eat self-service food in **disposable** containers with plastic forks. In my opinion, the overall solution to

---

[1] *market share:* the amount that a company sells of its products or services compared with other companies selling the same things

[2] *décor:* the style in which the interior of a building is decorated

[3] *waitstaff:* the people whose job is to serve customers at their tables in a restaurant

the problem of competition is to strengthen the welcoming, casual feeling of the restaurant.

My first recommendation is to update the interior décor. Even an inexpensive change such as fresh paint can make a dramatic difference. First, they could change the outdated yellow and orange color **scheme** to more relaxing colors. There is some risk because not all customers may like the new colors. But for a small investment, the owners can update and transform the interior. In addition, they might want to change the decorative art to make it more appealing to college students. For example, they could perhaps display student photographs, changing the selection every few months. Again, like painting, decorative art is an inexpensive change. A new interior **scheme** would highlight the relaxed atmosphere in contrast to the bright, noisy interior of the supermarket food court.

The next recommendation is to improve customer service. Excellent service is at the heart of any successful restaurant. **Negative** reviews cited problems with slow service and waitstaff that was not well trained. The Garcías have had ongoing problems **retaining** workers since most employees are students who come and go with the school year. Since the turnover rate[4] is high, the owners are hesitant to address poor job performance and **terminate** employees when necessary. Instead, the owners wait and hope the employee quits at the end of the school year. My recommendation involves a solution that will take time and energy: a more rigorous[5] hiring and training program **whereby protocols** are established for hiring and training staff. Guidelines for how employees should converse and interact with customers would also be helpful. Staff training takes time and may not result in a quick improvement in sales. In the long run, however, staff training will likely result in better customer service and satisfaction. It will also greatly improve employees' performance and job satisfaction.

Overall, Burger Corner is a well-established business, but changing the interior décor and improving customer service will strengthen and grow the business. By implementing these changes, Burger Corner will be able to attract and **retain** more customers, earning their loyalty, which should ultimately lead to higher profits.

---

[4] *turnover rate:* the rate at which employees leave a company and are replaced by other people
[5] *rigorous:* done carefully with a lot of attention to detail

WRITING SKILL   Problem and Solution

LEARN

In a case analysis, the writer focuses on the most critical problem(s) facing a business. The writer may either offer one solution or identify several possible solutions and recommend the best one. Usually there is no one correct solution because, in real life, there are various ways to solve a problem. When you write a business case analysis, follow these steps:

1. Provide background information about the business. Explain why the situation is worthy of analysis.

2. Identify the problems facing the business and identify one or two to focus on.

3. Explain the causes of, or what led to, those problem(s).

4. Present reasonable and attainable solutions and recommendations.

5. Comment on weaknesses or risks in your proposed solution(s). Any solution carries some risk that it will not work out as hoped.

Optional: Include an alternative solution but explain why it is not your first choice.

APPLY

A. Read the business case analysis on pages 110–112 again. Identify each item below as a problem (*P*), solution (*S*), or neither (*X*).

_P_ 1. Sales have decreased by 20 percent.

____ 2. The restaurant has a very good location.

____ 3. The food court at the new supermarket is busy and impersonal.

____ 4. Online reviews noted that service was slow and the décor was outdated.

____ 5. The owners can emphasize what is special about their restaurant.

____ 6. The owners are hesitant to terminate employees who perform poorly.

____ 7. Better employee training will lead to better service and customer satisfaction.

____ 8. A new color scheme can improve the interior appearance.

B. Answer the questions. Then discuss your answers with a partner.

1. In the first paragraph, what information is given? List five topics.

_____

2. What two specific changes does the writer suggest for the décor?

_____

3. What solution(s) does the writer offer for the problem of poor customer service?

_____

Analyze

A. Complete the diagram to show how the problems are connected. Use the phrases in the box.

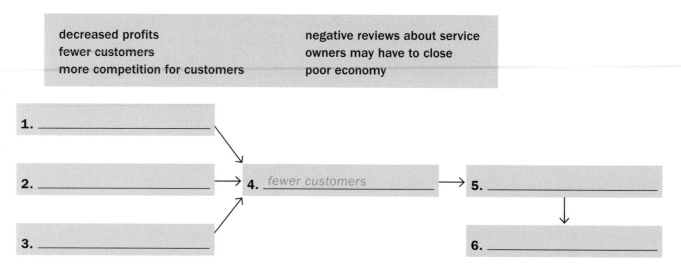

decreased profits
fewer customers
more competition for customers

negative reviews about service
owners may have to close
poor economy

1. _____

2. _____

3. _____

4. *fewer customers* _____

5. _____

6. _____

B. Number the items below to show the order of each paragraph.

____ 1. reason 1 for the declining business

____ 2. provide general background information about the business

____ 3. reason 2 for the declining business

____ 4. second recommendation relating to employee training

____ 5. explanation of why this situation is a serious problem for the owners

____ 6. first recommendation relating to the interior décor

____ 7. overall recommendation to strengthen what is good about the restaurant

C. Answer the questions. Then share your answers in a small group.

1. Reread the first two paragraphs of the case analysis. What words does the writer use to communicate the seriousness of the problem?

2. A case analysis should present reasonable and workable solutions. Do you think that improving the interior décor is a reasonable solution? Why, or why not?

3. What solution did the writer propose that is a long-term solution? Do you think this is a good recommendation? Why, or why not?

4. Of the recommendations made, which one does the writer seem less certain about? What language does the writer use to communicate a lack of confidence in the outcome of the solution?

5. Think of one other solution for the problems presented in the case.

A. Complete the Word Form Chart with the missing forms. Use a dictionary to check your answers.

Word Form Chart			
Noun	**Verb**	**Adjective**	**Adverb**
	compensate		_____
	convene		
	expose		_____
	negate		

B. Complete the paragraph using the correct form of the words in the chart.

(1) _____ wisdom would say that with high unemployment rates, a good employee should be easy to find. However, there are several problems for small retailers. First of all, many cannot offer the (2) _____ paid by large retail chains. Second, even if small retailers can match the salary, they usually cannot offer the same benefits. Poor health benefits are a(an) (3) _____ factor when considering a job offer. To counter these (4) _____, small retailers need to stress the advantages of working for a smaller company, like more on-the-job training and more chances for advancement. In a small business, employees are (5) _____ to all aspects of the operation, giving them a better understanding of the business.

Read the meanings of *expose* and notice the collocations.

1. to show the truth; collocations: *fully*, *clearly*, *publicly*

   The manager's report <u>clearly **exposed**</u> the lack of careful accounting in the store.

2. to cause someone to be affected by something harmful; collocations: *directly*, *constantly*, *regularly*

   TV ads <u>regularly **expose**</u> children to inappropriate images and messages.

3. to let someone experience an idea, feeling, situation, etc., usually a new one

   Students <u>were **exposed**</u> to many different types of customers.

CORPUS

C. Complete the sentences with the correct form of the word *expose*.

1. Restaurant reviews can _____ problems that managers may be unaware of.

2. Eric's business trip to China last year _____ him to different management styles.

3. Workers who are regularly _____ to harmful chemicals should follow all safety precautions.

4. A manager should not publicly _____ an employee's mistakes but should discuss the problems in private.

The noun *index* has several meanings. The traditional plural is *indices*, but *indexes* has also become an accepted plural.

1. a list of names or topics that are referred to in a book, usually arranged in alphabetical order at the end of the book

   *Consulting an **index** is a quick way to find specific information in a book.*

2. a system that shows the level of prices, pay, and so on, so that they can be compared with those of a previous date

   *Two common stock **indices** are the Dow Jones **Index** and the New York Stock Exchange **Index**.*

3. a sign or measure that something else can be judged by

   *Retail sales are a good **index** of consumer confidence and mood.*

CORPUS

D. Complete the sentences with a form of *index* and your own ideas.

1. My textbook has an _____. I use it when I _____.

2. The cost of living is a good _____ of _____.

3. A financial analyst usually follows the stock _____ very closely in

   order to _____.

4. An economist will study many financial _____ in order to

   understand the markets in areas of the world such as _____.

Vocabulary Activities | STEP II: Sentence Level

Whereby is a formal adverb meaning "by which" or "because of which."

   *They have started a new program **whereby** all employees must attend monthly training.*

CORPUS

E. Combine the two sentences into one sentence. Use *whereby*.

1. There is a standard health law. All employers are held responsible for their employees washing their hands.

   There is a standard health law whereby all employers are held responsible for their

   employees washing their hands.

2. They introduced a new business scheme. Students could get tutoring online at any time of day or night.

   _____

3. An alternative plan was presented. The new store would have self-service checkout counters.

   _____

Immigrate is a verb meaning "to come and live permanently in a country after leaving your own country." *Immigration* is a noncount noun that means "the process of coming to live in a country that is not your own." *Immigration* can also refer to "the place at an airport where passports and other documents of people coming into a country are checked." *Immigrant* is "a person who has come to live permanently in a country that is not his or her own."

He was born in Brazil. He **immigrated** to England. In England, he is a Brazilian **immigrant**.

 CORPUS

F. Answer the questions. Use a form of the word *immigrate*. Then share your answers in a small group.

1. Which foreign nationalities are the most common in your city?

   _____

2. How have immigration patterns in your country changed since 1960?

   _____

3. How do people of other cultures contribute to the well-being of a country?

   _____

G. Answer the questions. Use the target vocabulary in parentheses.

1. What is the main language spoken in businesses in your area? In your home? (dominant)

   _____

2. What strategies can a convenience store use to keep customers? (retain)

   _____

3. What might cause a company to fire an employee? (terminate)

_____

4. Fast-food restaurants create a lot of trash. How can they reduce the amount of plastic trash? (disposable)

_____

5. How can a beach-front hotel protect its property from storm damage? (erosion)

_____

6. What are some of the popular new business ideas these days? (schemes)

_____

7. When you have an official meeting of a committee, you follow certain rules and procedures. What are some examples in a typical meeting? (protocol)

_____

Grammar | Modals and Adverbs for Hedging

When writing a recommendation, you usually cannot state with 100-percent certainty that your idea will work. Also, there may be other solutions. Therefore, it is important to use _hedging_, or language that allows some uncertainty. With hedging, you can adjust the strength and certainty of your statements.

Notice the difference that hedging makes in each of the sentence pairs:

Painting is an inexpensive change, but it makes a dramatic difference.

Painting is an inexpensive change, but it _generally_ makes a dramatic difference. (hedging)

Painting is an inexpensive change, but it will make a dramatic difference.

Painting is an inexpensive change, but it _can often_ make a dramatic difference. (hedging)

Modals reflect different degrees of certainty. When you hedge, use modals that are somewhat certain and less certain.

Very certain	Somewhat certain	Less certain
will / won't	_can_	_may / might / could_

The following adverbs are useful in hedging. They express different degrees of certainty. Note that adverbs of frequency (_often_, _usually_, _sometimes_) go after a modal. Other adverbs listed can go before or after the modal.

certainly, completely, definitely, clearly, thoroughly, likely, probably, possibly, perhaps, conceivably, often, usually, sometimes

    v.   adv.   adv.   v.

It _can certainly_ make a difference. It _certainly can_ make a difference. (Adverb makes the modal stronger and can come before or after the modal.)

It _could perhaps_ make a difference. (Adverb makes the modal weaker.)

A. **Revise each sentence to make it less certain. More than one answer is possible.**

will likely give

1. New interior lighting ~~will give~~ a softer, more relaxed atmosphere.

2. Ads in the student newspaper introduce new students to the cafe.

3. An inexpensive daily lunch special leads to more lunchtime customers.

4. Discount coupons do not result in more sales over the long term.

5. Customer service will improve if waitstaff is better trained.

B. **Read the paragraph. Then revise it by using modals and adverbs for hedging.**

According to a recent news article, a major men's wear retailer has convened a series of meetings with investors and top-level officers to discuss the future direction of the company. It was founded about 30 years ago, but it has grown into a nationwide chain of stores that dominates the market of men's suits. Here are a few of my own recommendations for this business. First, it will increase its sales if it adds tuxedo rentals for men. Men have to rent tuxedos for weddings and other special occasions, and they look for an inexpensive way to do this. By having the rental department within the clothing store, customers will trust that the tuxedos will have the same level of quality as the store. Second, it will attract a broader range of customers if it diversifies its merchandise. By offering more casual business clothing, it will appeal to younger or less traditional customers.

WRITING SKILL　Evaluation

LEARN

A case analysis concludes with an evaluation of the recommendations. When you evaluate, consider the criteria for evaluation.

In business, the criteria for a good solution include the following:

- cost-effective (It will make more money than it costs.)
- practical (It can be implemented.)
- attainable (It is likely to succeed.)

Using these criteria, you can evaluate the strengths and weaknesses of your recommendations.

1. Evaluate your idea(s) using the criteria. Explain why yours is a good solution.

2. Discuss any weaknesses using the criteria. Use hedging language to express any uncertainty you have about your recommendation.

3. You may want to introduce one or two additional solutions and explain why they are not as effective. This will show that you have considered more than one solution, and it will make your recommendation stronger.

APPLY

Look at how evaluation is used in the business analysis on pages 110–112.

1. Complete the information from the sixth paragraph.

   First recommendation: _____ *update the interior décor* _____

   Strengths: _____

   Risk: _____

   Second recommendation: _____

   Strengths: _____

   Hedging language: _____

2. There are no specific risks mentioned for the second recommendation above. Think of a possible problem and complete the sentence.

   This plan, however, may be unreasonable because

   _____

   _____

   _____.

Collaborative Writing

A. Work as a class. Brainstorm three additional solutions to the problems of *Burger Corner*. Your criteria are that the solutions be practical and attainable.

1. *Offer daily lunch specials that are inexpensive and can be served quickly.*

2. _____

3. _____

4. _____

B. Discuss the strengths and weaknesses of each of the solutions in activity A. Select the two best solutions. For each one, complete notes to evaluate the solution.

Solution 1

Problem that it addresses: _____

Recommendation: _____

Strengths: _____

Weaknesses or risks: _____

Solution 2

Problem that it addresses: _____

Recommendation: _____

Strengths: _____

Weaknesses or risks: _____

C. In a small group, write a final paragraph of recommendation and evaluation to add to the business case analysis on pages 110–112. Choose one solution from activity B. Use hedging language.

1. Start your paragraph with "My final recommendation to Burger Corner is to ..."

2. Use target vocabulary words when possible, such as *compensation, dominate, erode, exposed, negative, retain,* and *terminate*.

D. Evaluate your paragraph. Does your solution meet the criteria of being practical and attainable? Answer these questions.

1. Is there information about strengths?

2. Are weaknesses mentioned?

3. Is hedging language used?

4. Is a weaker solution mentioned to show that other solutions were considered?

Independent Writing

A. You are going to write a business case analysis. A business case analysis presents a difficult problem (or problems) facing a business, explains the situation, and offers possible solutions. Think of a local business that has a problem that can be solved in a practical and reasonable way. Here are some ideas. Add your own ideas and notes about the problems.

1. A local restaurant that you are familiar with: _____

   Problem: _____

   _____

2. Your school cafeteria or bookstore: _____

   Problem: _____

   _____

3. A sports stadium or arena: _____

   Problem: _____

   _____

4. Your own idea: _____

   Problem: _____

   _____

B. Select one business for your case analysis. Check (✓) the specific problems that the business has. Add your own notes. Then consider how your solution can solve the most critical problem(s).

- ☐ changing consumer tastes
- ☐ competition from online businesses
- ☐ geographical location
- ☐ high prices
- ☐ lack of customer loyalty
- ☐ new competitor
- ☐ poor customer service
- ☐ staff turnover
- ☐ _____
- ☐ _____

C. Plan your case analysis. Complete the chart with notes.

Business name	
Background information	
Problem(s)	
Causes of the problems	
Solutions and specific recommendations	
Evaluation including strengths and weaknesses	
Additional solution and evaluation (optional)	

D. Complete the following sentences about your case study. Use the correct prepositions.

1. In order for _____ to compete _____,
_____.

2. Some customers have complained _____
_____.

3. One way to deal _____ the ongoing problem of _____
_____.

4. I recommend that the owners invest _____ because
_____.

5. It is not a good idea to rely _____ since
_____.

> **VOCABULARY TIP**
>
> Use these phrasal verbs to describe problems and changes. Notice the preposition that often follows each verb:
>
> *adjust to, come up with, compete with, complain about, deal with, deviate from, find out, invest in, react to, rely on, result in*

E. Write your business case analysis. Include a clear description of the business and the situation, the problem, your solution, and your evaluation of your solution. Your solution should fit the criteria of being cost-effective, practical, and attainable. Include hedging language. Use target vocabulary from page 109.

REVISE AND EDIT

A. Read your case analysis. Answer the questions below, and make revisions to your case analysis as needed.

1. Check (✓) the information you included in your case analysis.

   ☐ background information about the business

   ☐ explanation of the problem

   ☐ solutions and specific recommendations

   ☐ evaluation of strengths and weaknesses in terms of the criteria

2. Look at the information you did not include. Would adding that information make your case analysis more complete?

Grammar for Editing | Prepositions

Errors with prepositions may not interfere with the reader's understanding, but in academic writing, readers do not expect this sort of minor error. Because the use of prepositions is more idiomatic than rule-based, it is important to memorize which prepositions are used with which words. This is especially important with phrasal verbs, which are verbs with one or two prepositions.

When you edit your writing, check that each verb has the correct preposition with it. If you are not sure, check in a learners' dictionary. Different prepositions change the meaning of a verb phrase.

for
The city is known as its seafood restaurants.

as
New York is also known for the "Big Apple."

B. Check the language in your case analysis. Revise and edit as needed.

Language Checklist
☐ I used target words in my case analysis.
☐ I used phrasal verbs to describe problems and change.
☐ I used modals and adverbs to show hedging.
☐ I used correct prepositions with phrasal verbs.

C. Check your case analysis again. Repeat activities A and B.

Self-Assessment Review: Go back to page 109 and reassess your knowledge of the target vocabulary. How has your understanding of the words changed? What words do you feel most comfortable using now?

UNIT

9

Robots and Smart Machines

In this unit, you will

> analyze an exploratory essay and learn how it is used in academic writing.
> use discussion techniques to explain two sides of an issue.
> increase your understanding of the target academic words for this unit.

WRITING SKILLS

> Discussing Two Sides of an Issue
> Delayed Thesis
> **GRAMMAR** Real and Unreal Conditionals

Self-Assessment

Think about how well you know each target word, and check (✓) the appropriate column. I have…

TARGET WORDS	never seen this word before.	heard or seen the word but am not sure what it means.	heard or seen the word and understand what it means.	used the word confidently in *either* speaking or writing.
AWL				
albeit				
append				
🔑 bond				
complement				
confer				
🔑 convert				
dimension				
entity				
finite				
forthcoming				
invoke				
paradigm				
🔑 sector				
subordinate				

🔑 Oxford 3000™ keywords

Building Knowledge

Read these questions. Discuss your answers in a small group.

1. A robot is a machine that can perform a complicated series of tasks automatically. What kinds of tasks can a robot do?

2. How are robots used in manufacturing?

3. How do robots take away jobs from humans?

Writing Model

In an exploratory essay, the writer examines an issue by discussing both sides of it and closing with an evaluation. The exploratory mode of writing can be used in an academic setting, at work, or in a magazine article. Read this student essay exploring the issue of robotics.

Robots and Smart Machines

Robots have long been the subjects of science fiction novels. They are often portrayed as either helpful companions of the future or destructive evildoers from another **dimension**. In movies, robots are
5 humanlike **entities**, capable of reasoning and showing emotions. In the real world, robots may not reason or show emotions yet, but they are already incredibly complex. There are robots that can play games with a child, hand out flyers at a trade **conference**, win a
10 quiz game, or help an elderly person. Some robots even look like humans, **albeit** strange ones, with arms stiffly **appended**. They may not be attractive, but they are very smart and useful. Psychologists have noted that people even form emotional **bonds** to robots. In addition to
15 robots, which perform physical tasks, there are new so-called "smart machines." These are powerful computers capable of thinking, learning, and making decisions. In today's world, robots and smart machines are becoming more and more common, especially in the workplace.
20 The question is whether their impact on future jobs will be positive or negative.

Robots in movies

  The answer may be a little of both. As with all major advancements in technology, change brings great **paradigm** shifts. For example, when cars were first invented, no one could
25 imagine a day without the horse and carriage. Yet the age of the automobile has brought changes that few in the 1800s could have imagined. In the same way,

great innovations have led to robots that few imagined possible 50 years ago. The field of robots is booming.[1] The result is rapid change, not just in manufacturing, but also in every **sector** of the global economy. For this reason, a thoughtful
30 exploration of the future impact of robots and smart machines is important. Some see them as having a positive impact, whereas others see them as decidedly negative.

Robots in manufacturing

Experts in the high-tech **sector** see the
35 benefits of using robots and smart machines. They believe that these innovations will bring positive changes for employees. In manufacturing and industry, robots can do mechanical tasks more quickly and accurately
40 than human workers, generating higher profits for companies. With robots doing the lower-level jobs, more employees will move up to higher-level jobs. According to this positive view, workers will have better and more
45 interesting jobs in the future, thanks to robots and smart machines.

Many see this as the bright promise of the future—enhancing the quality of life through better jobs. People will have higher-paid jobs, resulting in more money to spend and a positive effect on the economy. Work can be done more efficiently, with robots doing the repetitive or physically difficult jobs. For
50 example, a warehouse worker can direct a robot to do all of the heavy lifting. Smart machines, which process and analyze large amounts of data quickly, will reduce errors and improve efficiency. Watson, IBM's supercomputer, is **invoked** as a symbol of the most powerful smart machine. It became famous by winning a popular TV quiz show. Watson is now assisting doctors by quickly analyzing huge
55 quantities of data. Watson helps doctors make the best choices about medications and treatments. Like Watson, smart machines will be the new **subordinates** in the office, managed by professionals. The future possibilities seem almost **infinite**. When we view robots and smart machines as tools that can **complement** our own job skills, we can see the long-term benefits of embracing this change.

60 On the other side, many economic and employment experts are more pessimistic[2] about the impact of robots and smart machines. There is a great concern that robots will continue to displace[3] large numbers of low-skilled workers.[4] As factories are **converted** to robotic manufacturing, some fear that more low-skilled workers will become unemployed. According to the 2012
65 McKinsey Global Institute report, by 2020, developing countries could have 58 million unemployed low-skilled workers. Most will have been replaced by automation. The problem is that unemployed workers are not finding new jobs. Technology is changing the workplace at such a fast rate that workers have not been able to adjust quickly enough.

---

[1] *booming:* having a period of rapid growth
[2] *pessimistic:* expecting bad things to happen
[3] *displace:* take the place of someone
[4] *low-skilled workers:* workers who need minimal training, experience, or education to do their jobs

70　　　With **forthcoming** advances in technology, many skilled workers[5] will also lose their jobs. Even now, travel agents, phone operator, utility meter reader, and office assistant are becoming jobs of the past. "Most business and thought

75　leaders underestimate the potential of smart machines to take over millions of middle-class jobs in the coming decades," states Kenneth Brant, research director at Gartner, a global technology research firm. According to a recent Oxford

80　University study, up to 47 percent of all current jobs in the United States could be done by a robot or smart machine within the next 20 years.

People need to retrain to work with robots.

　　　Experts predict that if more workers lose their jobs and are unable to find new ones, unemployment rates will rise. Consequently, the global economy will

85　continue to struggle. In an Associated Press study of data from 20 countries, researchers found that millions of skilled jobs have been lost over a recent five-year period. These are significant job losses for the middle class in developed countries around the world. If job losses continue at this rate, the financial health of every country will suffer. In today's global economy, the economy of every

90　country matters. Experts fear that the rapid loss of low-skilled and skilled jobs will have a very negative impact on the global economy.

　　　Progress and innovation are inevitable and essential, but it is especially concerning that such large numbers of low-skilled workers are losing their jobs. If this were a perfect world, these workers would be retrained for more skilled

95　jobs. They would receive higher wages, and their higher incomes and increased spending would support the local economy. However, this is not happening. Unskilled workers who are forced out of the job market by robots are not finding new jobs because they are not being retrained. Robots deliver higher profits and support the economy. However, those profits are not reinvested into training

100　workers for skilled jobs. Instead, the profits increase the wealth of a small portion of the world population. The problem is not robots and smart machines. The problem is the failure to prepare low-skilled and skilled workers for the jobs of tomorrow. If this can be solved, robots and smart machines can truly benefit the world.

---

[5] *skilled workers:* workers who have specialized skill, knowledge, or ability for their jobs

LEARN

In some academic writing assignments, you will need to present two sides of an issue. In a discussion, the writer presents both sides in a balanced and objective way. The purpose is to explore an issue in depth. A discussion is often part of a longer assignment, such as an exploratory essay. To write a discussion of two sides of an issue, follow these steps:

- Start by presenting the issue and giving background information.

- Explain why it is a significant issue.

- Present the most convincing arguments for each position. Use reasons and examples. Describe each position in a respectful manner.

- You may point out what may motivate someone to take a position.

- You can follow each point with the opposing point. Alternatively, you can group all points for each side of the issue together.

- After the discussion, you may take a position on the issue.

APPLY

A. Read the statements below that summarize the essay on pages 126–128. Number the statements in the order of the discussion elements.

____ 1. To provide background, the writer gives examples of what robots do.

____ 2. The first position on the issue is that robots and smart machines will bring beneficial changes to future jobs and the economy.

____ 3. The topic is robots. The issue is their impact on jobs.

____ 4. After a discussion of both sides of the issue, the writer says that employers and educators need to make sure workers are trained for new jobs.

____ 5. The second position on the issue is that the impact on workers and future jobs will be quite negative.

____ 6. Some people view the impact as positive, while others believe the impact will be negative.

____ 7. Because changes in technology are happening so quickly, every sector of the economy is affected. For that reason, this is an important topic.

B. Work with a partner. Discuss each statement and decide if it could be added to the essay on pages 126–128. If so, where could it be added and how would it add to the discussion? If not, why is it not appropriate to add?

1. According to the International Federation of Robotics, the global annual sales of industrial robots increased by 25 percent between 2005 and 2012.

2. This is not surprising because high-tech professionals always think that technology is the best solution for every problem.

3. When automobiles replaced horses and carriages, many workers initially lost their jobs. Most found new jobs in manufacturing. Today, however, changes are happening so rapidly that workers are unable to attain new job skills.

Analyze

A. Complete the outline for each side of the issue.

Side 1: People with a positive viewpoint (for example,

people in the high-tech sector)

A. Robots can bring positive changes.

   1. Robots can _____.

   2. Workers will _____.

B. If robots are widely used, people will have _____.

   1. Workers will _____.

   2. Robots can _____.

C. Smart machines can _____.

   1. Example of Watson: _____.

   2. Professional workers will _____.

Conclusion for Side 1: _____

Side 2: People with a negative viewpoint (for example, _____)

D. Robots will _____.

   1. 58 million _____.

   2. Unemployed low-skilled workers _____.

   3. _____ is changing so quickly that _____.

E. Medium-skilled workers _____.

   1. Examples of types of jobs lost: _____.

   2. In our global economy, _____.

Conclusion for Side 2: _____

B. Reread the last paragraph of the essay on page 128 and answer the questions.

1. In the last paragraph, the writer begins an evaluation of the issue. How does the first sentence acknowledge points made on each side of the issue?

   _____

2. What verb forms does the writer use to talk about possible future conditions?

   _____

3. In the writer's viewpoint, what is the critical problem and what is a solution?

   _____

C. Discuss these questions with a small group.

1. Do you agree with the writer's opinion about the issue? In other words, do you agree that it is a serious problem that will have a negative impact?

2. The writer states: "The problem is not robots and smart machines. The problem is the failure to prepare low-skilled and skilled workers for the jobs of tomorrow." Do you agree? Why, or why not?

3. How might robots and smart machines impact your career in the future?

4. How do you think robots can improve your home life in the future?

Vocabulary Activities STEP I: Word Level

A. Complete the Word Form Chart. Use a dictionary to check your answers. Compare your answers with a partner.

Word Form Chart			
Noun	**Verb**	**Adjective**	**Adverb**
	append	_____	_____
	confer	_____	_____
	convert		_____
subordination			

B. Complete the paragraph using the correct form of the words in the chart.

The company will (1) _____ the old factory into a modern one

with a fully robotic manufacturing process. In this factory, the new

(2) _____ will be robots, not people. Managers will oversee

technical issues rather than issues related to managing people. After the

factory-planning meeting, the two architects (3) _____ for several

minutes behind closed doors. In the forthcoming design report, there will be

several drawings of the proposed design changes in the (4) _____.

C. Complete the paragraph using words from the box.

bonds	dimension	entity	forthcoming	paradigm	sector

Over the past several years, there has been a new (1) _____ for

integrating students with medical problems into the classroom. In the past, if

a student were unable to attend school due to a long-term medical condition,

the student would receive tutoring at home. Now, a sick student can use a

videoconferencing robot to "attend" school. Students are able to maintain

social (2) _____ with classmates because they have a virtual

presence at school every day. This adds a very positive (3) _____ to

an otherwise isolated time. The student's classmates quickly accept the robot

as the student's representative, not just an electronic (4) _____.

Changes to the education (5) _____ came about after

telecommuters transformed the business world. What other changes are

(6) _____?

Complement, which can be a verb or a noun, is often confused with the word
compliment, also a verb and noun.

Complement (verb) means "to add to something in a way that improves it."
A *complement* (noun) to something is "a thing that adds new qualities to
something to improve it or make it more attractive."

A computer can **complement** learning that takes place outside of the classroom.

A laptop is a necessary **complement** to classroom learning.

Compliment (verb) means "to tell someone that you like or admire something
he or she has done." The noun *compliment* is "a remark that expresses praise
or admiration."

My teacher **complimented** me on my computer skills.

Thank you for the nice **compliment**.

CORPUS

D. Complete the sentences with the correct noun or verb form of *complement* or *compliment*.

1. I use a full _____ of software programs in my statistics course.

2. My manager rarely _____ me on my work, so his praise yesterday was encouraging.

3. The two engineers work well together because their different skills _____ each other.

4. Although I meant my remark as a _____, I could see that the young boy was offended by it.

5. Wind energy can be a _____ to energy from oil and coal.

6. A robot tour guide could _____ the experience for the museum visitor.

7. It is difficult to give my uncle a _____ because he always turns it into a joke or an insult.

Invoke is a verb with several specific meanings and uses. It often is used in the passive voice.

1. to mention or use a law, rule, etc., as a reason for doing something

   *It is unlikely that the new law will be **invoked** in this situation.*

2. to mention a person, a theory, an example, etc., to support your opinion or idea or as a reason for something

   *She **invoked** several experts to back up her argument.*

3. to mention someone's name to make people feel a particular thing or act in a particular way

   *His name was **invoked** as a symbol of a compassionate scientist.*

CORPUS

E. Complete the sentences with the correct form of *invoke*. Note if the usage is definition *1, 2,* or *3*.

____ 1. The name of Dr. Martin Luther King, Jr. _____ in most speeches about civil rights in the United States.

____ 2. During the discussion, Ramon _____ the name of several experts, but we were not familiar with them and we remain unimpressed.

____ 3. When the woman was arrested, she _____ her right to remain silent until she had a lawyer with her.

Finite is an adjective meaning "having a definite limit or a fixed size." For example, you can have a finite number of things.

Infinite, with the negative prefix *in-*, means "without limits; without end." *Infinite* can also mean "very great." The adverb *infinitely* means "very much" or "extremely; with no limit."

CORPUS

F. Write sentences using the correct form of *finite* or *infinite*. Some possible collocations are given in parentheses.

1. Compare a new computer with old computer (faster; better)

   _____

2. Software applications for a cell phone (variety; number of)

   _____

3. Earth's resources (supply)

   _____

4. Job opportunities (number of)

   _____

Albeit is a formal conjunction meaning "although" or "though." It is usually used to introduce a phrase that reduces the effect of what you said just before it.

> *Their robot was the fastest, **albeit** the smallest, contestant in the student competition.*

> *The videoconferencing software was a great improvement, **albeit** very expensive.*

CORPUS

G. Combine the sentence pairs into one sentence. Use *albeit*.

1. The importance of face-to-face meetings is part of an valid paradigm. It is still a valid paradigm.

   The importance of face-to-face meetings is part of an old, albeit valid, paradigm.

2. It was a very short journal article. It was important.

   _____

3. The researchers found a good solution to the lab problem. It was a temporary solution.

   _____

Grammar | Real and Unreal Conditionals

In a conditional statement, the *if*-clause, or "conditional clause," expresses the possibility, and the main clause expresses the result. The conditional clause does not always begin with *if*. It can also be introduced with *when, unless, as long as,* or *even if.*

1. For the real conditional, use simple present for facts, general truths, and causes in the conditional clause. Use simple present in the main clause.

   conditional clause=possibility   main clause=result
   _If_ unemployment _rises_, the economy usually _suffers_.

2. For predictions or possibilities in the future, use simple present in the conditional clause. Use future time (*will, be going to*) and modals in the main clause.

   conditional clause=possibility   main clause=future result
   _If_ I _lose_ my job, I _could have_ a difficult time finding another one.

3. Use the unreal conditional to describe a situation that is not true in the present or to speculate about the future. Use the past form of the verb in the conditional clause. Use *were* for all forms of *be* in the conditional clause. In the main clause, use the modals *would, could,* or *might* + verb.

   conditional-clause=unreal possibility   main clause=speculation about future result
   _If_ I _were working full time at a good job_, I _would have_ enough money for a car.

A. Read the sentences from the writing model. Underline the subject and circle the verb in each clause. Then write whether the sentence expresses a real conditional for a *general truth* or for a *possibility in the future* or an *unreal conditional.*

1. Experts predict that if more workers lose their jobs and are unable to find new ones, unemployment rates will rise. _____

2. If this were a perfect world, these workers would be retrained for more skilled jobs. _____

3. When we view robots as tools that can complement our own job skills, we can see the long-term benefits of embracing this change. _____

B. Complete the sentences in your own words. Use the unreal conditional. Explain how your life would be different if you had different abilities, and so on.

1. (different abilities) _____ *If I were a better soccer player, I would join your team.*

2. (different nationality) _____

3. (different age) _____

4. (different city of residence) _____

5. (different education level)_____

WRITING SKILL | Delayed Thesis

LEARN

In many types of writing, it works best to state a thesis at the beginning of an essay. For example, in an argument essay, a thesis at the beginning gives the reader a preview of the writer's argument. It introduces the thesis and focuses the reader's attention on the issue.

However, there are other situations where it is more appropriate to delay the thesis. For example, in an exploratory essay, start by presenting background information about the issue or topic. Then guide the reader through a balanced discussion of both sides of the issue. After the discussion section, evaluate the strength of each side. Finally, give your thesis and state your position. This is called a delayed thesis.

APPLY

Answer the questions about the essay on pages 126–128.

1. In which paragraph can you find the delayed thesis? _____

2. In the paragraph with the delayed thesis, the writer includes points from the discussion section and then adds a personal opinion or perspective. Complete the chart below. Restate the writer's evaluation of the discussion points.

Point from the discussion section	Writer's response or point of view
a. Many people are losing jobs because of robots and smart machines.	*This is a very concerning situation.*
b. Unskilled workers should receive training for new jobs.	
c. Robots are very efficient, so companies are more productive and earn higher profits.	
d. The economy will grow because of greater productivity with robots and smart machines.	

3. In your own words, what is the writer's thesis?

_____

_____

Collaborative Writing

A. Work with a partner. Read the student notes for a different final paragraph for the essay on page 128. Read the sentences and number them to show the best order for an alternative concluding paragraph.

___ 1. For example, jobs related to horses and carriages that were lost due to the automobile were eventually replaced.

___ 2. In the same way, robots and smart machines will undoubtedly displace workers. But these workers will find new jobs in the future.

___ 3. The change took time, but eventually almost all of the displaced workers found work in the automotive industry.

___ 4. While I share the concerns of those who feel that robots and smart machines will result in more unemployment, I have a more optimistic view.

___ 5. Additionally, I feel sure that the new jobs will be better and more satisfying.

___ 6. A long-term view of global unemployment trends shows that the overall unemployment rate is remarkably stable. Although some jobs are lost, others are eventually created.

B. Work with a partner. Write two different concluding sentences for the paragraph in activity A. Each one will include a delayed thesis statement. Then choose the strongest sentence.

Concluding sentence 1: _____

_____

Concluding sentence 2: _____

_____

C. Work together to write a new final paragraph for the writing model on pages 126–128. Use the sentences from activity A and your delayed thesis statement. Add additional information or make changes as you wish.

D. Compare your paragraph with another pair's. Discuss these questions.

1. Does the paragraph start by giving the writer's general viewpoint?

2. Does the paragraph include points from the discussion section?

3. Does the paragraph use thoughtful and balanced language?

4. Is the thesis statement clear? How can you improve it?

Independent Writing

A. You are going to write an exploratory essay. First, read the student notes about automation in customer service. Answer the questions to prepare to write an exploratory essay in which you will discuss both sides of an issue.

1. What information would you include as background about the topic? Mark it with a check (✓).

2. Which statements would not be useful in a discussion of both sides of the issue? Why not? Mark them with an X.

3. What ideas can you add to the notes?

> Automation in customer service
> Examples: automated phone systems to get information (for example, about your account or about a reservation); self check-out cash registers in stores; automated banking services; automated food service in the future; no waiters or waitresses—send food order electronically from the table?
> Automation—more efficient and faster than talking with a real person
> Some customers prefer automation
> Disadvantages of automation?
> Human interaction is important.
> Automation saves companies money; workers don't have to do boring jobs.
> Automated phone systems are so frustrating to me!
> When customers need assistance, they prefer talking with a real person.

B. Organize your ideas for a discussion of both sides of the issue of automation in customer service. Use the notes in activity A and add other information such as examples. If necessary, conduct additional research on the issue.

Side 1: Automation is _____.	Side 2: Automation is _____.

C. Answer the questions to plan your writing.

1. In your opening paragraph, what background information will you include?

   _____

2. Which issue will you put first? Why? _____

3. Write three conditional statements to use in your exploratory essay.

   a. Real conditional about a general truth: _____

   b. Real conditional about a possibility in the future: _____

   c. Unreal conditional: _____

4. Think about how you will evaluate the issues at the end of your essay. What

   will your delayed thesis be? _____

D. Complete the paragraph. Use the correct form of words from the Vocabulary Tip box.

> **VOCABULARY TIP**
>
> Use a variety of word forms to talk about automation:
>
> *automation, automate, automated, automatically*
>
> Useful technical words to talk about customer service:
>
> *keypad, menu options, robotic voice, scan, touch screen*

Most banks have ATMs, which are like (1) _____ bank tellers

that perform banking transactions. After inserting your card, use a

(2) _____ to type your password. Then select what type of

transaction you want. For example, you can deposit or withdraw money.

Some newer ATMs use a special monitor with a (3) _____. For

these, touch the monitor to select what kind of transaction you want.

There is usually a list of (4) _____ to choose from. Some

ATMs can now (5) _____ each check that you deposit. Your

deposit receipt shows an image of each check you have deposited. In addition

to ATMs, banks use (6) _____ customer service phone numbers.

A (7) _____ will ask you a series of questions. It may answer your

questions or connect you with a real person. (8) _____ has made

banking easier and more convenient.

E. Write your exploratory essay. Start with a discussion of both sides of the issue and end with your evaluation and delayed thesis. Use your planning notes and outline. In your writing, use target vocabulary from page 125.

A. Read your explanatory essay. Answer the questions below, and make revisions as needed.

1. Check (✓) the information you included in your exploratory essay.

   ☐ an introduction to the issue

   ☐ a balanced presentation of two sides of the issue

   ☐ an explanation of your own position

   ☐ background information

   ☐ support with examples and reasons

   ☐ a delayed thesis

2. Look at the information you did not include. Would adding that information make your essay more complete?

Grammar for Editing | Verb Tenses in Unreal Conditional Sentences

Check your writing for correct use of verb tenses in unreal conditional sentences in the present. Even though you are thinking about a future unreal situation, use past forms.

> If I _could order_ my groceries online for a good price, I _could stop_ going to the supermarket every week.

Note that for unreal conditional, _were_ is used for both singular and plural subjects.

> If I _were_ more familiar with the latest technology, I _would not be_ so hesitant to buy it.

B. Check the language in your essay. Revise and edit as needed.

Language Checklist
☐ I used target words in my exploratory essay.
☐ I used a variety of word forms to talk about automation and technical words to talk about customer service.
☐ I used real and unreal conditional sentences.
☐ I used correct verb tenses in unreal conditional sentences.

C. Check your exploratory essay again. Repeat activities A and B.

Self-Assessment Review: Go back to page 125 and reassess your knowledge of the target vocabulary. How has your understanding of the words changed? What words do you feel most comfortable using now?

UNIT 10

Digging through History

In this unit, you will

> analyze syntheses and learn how they are used in academic writing.

> use comparison and contrast to write about two articles.

> increase your understanding of the target academic words for this unit.

WRITING SKILLS

> Comparing and Contrasting Sources

> Introductions and Conclusions

> **GRAMMAR** Articles

Self-Assessment

Think about how well you know each target word, and check (✓) the appropriate column. I have...

TARGET WORDS	never seen this word before.	heard or seen the word but am not sure what it means.	heard or seen the word and understand what it means.	used the word confidently in *either* speaking or writing.
AWL				
administrate				
commodity				
denote				
discrete				
distinct				
🔑 emerge				
hierarchy				
infrastructure				
🔑 layer				
migrate				
🔑 parallel				
predominant				
🔑 trace				
transmit				

🔑 Oxford 3000™ keywords

Building Knowledge

Read these questions. Discuss your answers in a small group.

1. What do you know about the history of Mexico and Central America?

2. Which ancient cultures are you familiar with?

3. Do you think it is valuable to study cultures that no longer exist?

Writing Model

A synthesis is a summary of the similarities and differences between two sources. Read about a controversy over two ancient cultures, the Maya and the Olmec, who lived in Mesoamerica (Mexico and northern Central America).

The Mother Culture of Mesoamerica

Around 3,000 years ago, the earliest civilizations in Mesoamerica **emerged** in the area that is now Mexico and Guatemala. In particular, two advanced cultures developed—the Olmec and the Maya. However, scholars disagree over the relationship between those cultures. Some anthropologists,[1]
5 such as Jeffrey Blomster of George Washington University, argue that the

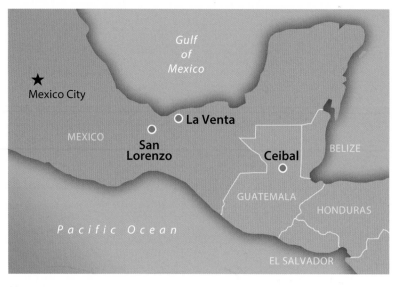

Mesoamerica

---

[1] *anthropologist:* a person who studies the origins, developments, customs, and beliefs of human societies

Olmec were the "mother culture" of the region and greatly influenced the Maya and other civilizations that followed them. Others, such as Takeshi Inomata at the University of Arizona, suggest that the Maya and the Olmec influenced each other. This
10 would make the Maya and the Olmec "sister" cultures. Recent archaeological research has reopened the debate about these two fascinating but little understood peoples.

Mayan statue

Inomata et al. (2013) agree with Blomster, Neff, and Glascock (2005) that the Olmec occupied the first major city in the region
15 near San Lorenzo, in modern-day Mexico. This city may have served as the capital of the Olmec civilization. There, they built colossal[2] stone sculptures, which still exist today. These figures probably **denoted** their **administrative** leaders. The Olmec had an organized political **hierarchy** and a thriving economy. San Lorenzo was an
20 impressive site because it was set on an artificial plateau[3] that the Olmec built for their major city. However, excavations[4] on the site of the former city reveal no evidence of a formal plan for the layout of the buildings. This development, which is typical of Mayan cities (Inomata et al., 2013), would come later.

Olmec statue

25 Although both teams of researchers describe the fall of San Lorenzo, they disagree over the date. According to Blomster et al. (2005), the Olmec abandoned San Lorenzo around 900 BCE,[5] whereas Inomata et al. (2013) estimate it was about 250 years earlier. However, it is not known why the Olmec left San Lorenzo. That
30 remains a mystery. The next major Olmec city is believed to have been La Venta. This served as the Olmecs' capital after they **migrated** from San Lorenzo. La Venta is located closer to the Gulf of Mexico and shows signs of developments in Olmec culture as well as more sophisticated **infrastructure**. For example, pyramids[6] have been found at La
35 Venta but not San Lorenzo. Blomster observes that the Maya built similar pyramids not long after the time that La Venta was founded. For this reason, he calls the Olmec the "mother culture" from which the Maya and other groups descended (Blomster et al., 2005). Evidence for this claim comes from pieces of pottery found at La Venta. When Blomster's team analyzed the
40 pottery fragments, they found chemicals that are **distinct** to the clay[7] around San Lorenzo, meaning that the pottery was probably made in San Lorenzo and sold to other places. Blomster also cites other archeologists who discovered artworks from San Lorenzo in ancient cities around the region. This suggests that San Lorenzo was the center for the trade of art and
45 **commodities** in the region at that time. As a result, Olmec style, knowledge, and skills were **transmitted** to other cultures such as the Maya.

---

[2] *colossal:* extremely large
[3] *plateau:* an area of flat land that is higher than the land around it
[4] *excavation:* the activity of digging in the ground to look for old buildings or objects that have been buried for a long time
[5] *BCE:* before the year 1 in the Western calendar
[6] *pyramid:* large building with a square or triangular base and sloping sides that meet in a point at the top
[7] *clay:* a type of heavy, sticky earth that becomes hard when it is baked and is used to make things such as pots and bricks

More recent excavations by Inomata and his colleagues, however, cast doubt on the **predominant** hypothesis. Inomata investigated the ancient Maya city of Ceibal, which is in present-day Guatemala. The Maya were famous for
50 rebuilding their cities, which often meant knocking down old structures and putting up new ones. By digging 12-meter-deep shafts[8] through the many **layers** of the city, Inomata was able to reach the oldest settlement at the site. There, his team found **traces** of the same arrangement of pyramids and public buildings as at La Venta. Importantly, scientific dating methods
55 strongly indicate that Ceibal was built after San Lorenzo but before La Venta. Since there are no pyramids at San Lorenzo, Inomata concludes that the Maya did not borrow this architectural style from the Olmec. In fact, the Olmec at La Venta may have borrowed it from the Maya at Ceibal. This would mean the Maya and the Olmec developed in **parallel** at about the same
60 time. That is, they are **discrete** cultures that influenced each other. Unlike Blomster, Inomata believes that the Maya and the Olmec are more like sisters than mother and daughter.

Inomata's article does not settle the matter, though. His findings do not explain why so many civilizations, including the Maya, turned to San Lorenzo
65 for trade. Blomster found no **traces** of any imports to San Lorenzo, only exports from the city, which for him confirms its importance as the most advanced artistic center of the region. Since San Lorenzo has not been fully excavated, it is also possible that Olmec pyramids will still be found there, pre-dating the ones at Ceibal. Furthermore, it is not known whether there
70 are other, older Olmec cities in the region that have disappeared. The truth about these fascinating ancient civilizations, among the oldest on the American continent, remains to be discovered. ■

REFERENCES

Blomster, J. P., Neff, H., & Glascock, M.D. (2005). Olmec pottery production and export in ancient Mexico determined through elemental analysis. *Science, 307,* 1068–1072.

Inomata, T., Triadan, D., Aoyama, K., Castillo, V., & Yonenobu, H. (2013). Early ceremonial constructions at Ceibal, Guatemala, and the origins of lowland Maya civilization. *Science, 340,* 467–471.

---

[8] *shaft:* a long, narrow, vertical hole dug as part of an excavation

Comparing and Contrasting Sources

LEARN

In a good synthesis, writers make connections between sources. Sources may agree in some ways but differ in others. One way to write about two sources is to summarize one article first and then the other. However, there may be too much repetition. Therefore, syntheses are usually either organized around key ideas or with similarities first, followed by differences.

When you write a synthesis, follow these steps:

1. Read the source articles carefully and take notes on the main ideas.

2. Understand the purpose of each source: Is it an argument, discussion, report, research paper, or narrative?

3. If the sources contain arguments, identify the authors' opinions.

4. Identify connections and similarities between the sources. Take notes.

5. Look for differences between the sources.

6. Organize your notes so you have a list of similarities and differences.

7. Use language to mark similarities and differences such as *in contrast, similarly, agree, disagree, like,* and *unlike.*

APPLY

A. Read the synthesis on pages 142–144 again. Answer the questions below.

1. Where did the Olmec and Maya live? _____

2. What was the relationship between them? _____

3. Why was San Lorenzo important? _____

4. When did the Olmec leave San Lorenzo? _____

5. Which culture first built pyramids and in which city? _____

6. Was San Lorenzo an importer or exporter or art and commodities? _____

B. Complete the Venn diagram with your answers from activity A. If the two sources agree on a fact or idea, write the idea in the middle section of the diagram. If only one source has that idea, write it under that source only.

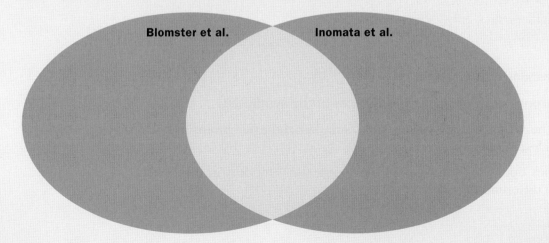

Blomster et al.   Inomata et al.

Analyze

A. Read the synthesis on page 142–144 again. Which sources does the writer use in each paragraph? Check the correct columns in the chart.

Paragraph	Blomster et al. (2005)	Inomata et al. (2013)
1	✓	✓
2		
3		
4		
5		

B. Write the number of the paragraph that has each function.

_1_ 1. introduces the two sources

___ 2. presents Blomster's main argument

___ 3. shows why further research is needed

___ 4. presents Inomata's main argument

___ 5. explains where Blomster and Inomata agree with each other

C. Underline the citations in the writing model. Find both types of citation.

a. Author is in sentence: Smith (2012) argues that …

b. Author is in parentheses: The problem is serious (Smith, 2012).

D. Use your answers in activity C to complete the chart. See page 97 for information about correctly citing sources.

	Author(s) in sentence	Author(s) in parentheses
One author	Smith (2012)	(Smith, 2012)
Two authors	Robins and Jones (2011)	(Robins & Jones, 2011)
Three authors, first citation only		(Blomster, Neff, & Glascock, 2005)
Three authors, subsequent citations		
Four to seven authors, first and subsequent citations		

E. Discuss the questions with a partner.

1. What is the purpose of the first three sentences of the synthesis?

2. Do you think the writer of the synthesis has summarized every point in both the source articles? Why, or why not?

3. What verb tenses does the writer use in the synthesis? Why do you think the writer uses the different tenses?

Word Form Chart		
Noun	**Adjective**	**Adverb**
discretion	discrete	discretely
indiscretion	discretionary	
distinction	distinct	distinctly
	indistinct	indistinctly
	distinctive	

A. Write the correct word form next to each definition. Some forms will not be used.

1. _____discrete_____ independent of each other

2. _____ clearly different or of a different kind

3. _____ the freedom or power to decide what should be done in a particular situation

4. _____ easily or clearly heard, seen, or felt

5. _____ having a quality or characteristic that makes something different

6. _____ cannot be seen, heard, or remembered clearly

7. _____ decided according to the judgment of a person in authority; not decided by rules

8. _____ the quality of being excellent, special, or important

9. _____ an act or remark that is not acceptable or that offends or embarrasses someone

B. Write the target word next to the category it describes. Add two more examples to each category.

administrator	commodity	hierarchy	infrastructure

1. _____ director, principal, governor, _____, _____

2. _____ gold, oil, rice, _____, _____

3. _____ highest to lowest, oldest to youngest, closest to farthest, _____, _____

4. _____ bridge, road, pipe, _____, _____

Trace can be a noun or a verb. As a noun, it has two primary uses,

1. a sign that someone was present or something existed in the past

   *Ancient civilizations have left **traces** of their cultures across the Americas.*

2. a very small amount of something

   *Soil in the region contains **traces** of lead.*

As a verb, it has four more meanings.

1. to find someone or something by looking carefully

   *The author of the anonymous letter **was traced** to Japan.*

2. to find the origin or cause of something

   *The design of the building **traces back** to the ancient Greeks.*

3. to describe a process or development

   *This article **traces** the history of the Maya until the fall of their empire.*

4. to make a copy of a shape by drawing around it or over it

   *The archaeologist carefully **traced** the drawings she found on the cave walls.*

CORPUS

C. Write sentences about the writing model using these phrases. You may change the tense of the verbs.

1. found no traces

   Archaeologists have found no traces of the lost city of Atlantis.

2. trace the history of

   _____

3. traces of

   _____

4. trace the first person who

   _____

5. left traces

   _____

6. trace the source of this information back

   _____

D. Write answers to the questions. Use a form of the target vocabulary in parentheses.

1. What is the most common language spoken in your school, town, region, or country? (predominant)

_____

2. What does a lack of eye contact mean in your culture? (denote)

_____

3. When did the Olmec culture first appear? (emerge)

_____

4. Why is it important to pass on traditions from one generation to the next? (transmit)

_____

5. What are some reasons for the movement of people between countries? (migration)

_____

6. What would future anthropologists find if they dug down to the level of our present day? (layer)

_____

Parallel can be an adjective, an adverb, a noun, or a verb.

1. As an adjective, it means "describing two or more lines that are the same distance apart at every point." It can also mean "very similar or taking place at the same time."

    The road and the canal are **parallel** to each other.

2. Parallel can be an adverb.

    The road and the canal run **parallel** to each other.

3. As a noun, it means "a person, situation, or event that is very similar to another."

    This tradition has no **parallel** in our country.

4. As a verb, it can mean "to be similar to something, to happen at the same time, or to be as good as something."

    The rise in employment is **paralleled** by an increase in home sales.

    His work, comprising 125,000 entries, has not been **paralleled**.

CORPUS

E. Write answers to the following questions. Use the form of *parallel* in parentheses in your answers.

1. Do you think there is an equivalent to the pyramids of ancient Egypt? (parallel to)

_____

2. What similarities are there between the Maya and the Olmec? (parallel – adj.)

_____

3. What parallels can you draw between archaeology and history? (parallels between)

_____

Grammar Articles

Articles are used to show whether a noun refers to one thing in particular, one thing out of many, or all members of a group. To use the correct article, you must know if the noun is countable or uncountable. Countable nouns can be plural; uncountable nouns cannot.

1. With uncountable and plural countable nouns, use no article except to show definite reference (*the*).

   <u>Anthropology</u> is the <u>study</u> of <u>human society</u>.
   uncountable   the <u>study</u>   uncountable
   definite

   <u>Commodities</u> were traded between <u>the major cities</u> of <u>the two civilizations</u>.
   plural   plural   plural
   definite   definite

2. Singular count nouns must have an article or a similar word (*this, my, his, one,* etc.). Use *the* when you mean one particular thing or idea that the reader already knows (definite); otherwise, use *a/an* (indefinite).

   <u>The first major city</u> in <u>the region</u> was built on <u>a plateau</u>.
   singular countable   singular countable   singular countable
   definite   definite   indefinite

   According to <u>a recent article</u>, <u>a distinct hierarchy</u> existed in <u>the culture</u>.
   singular countable   singular countable   singular countable
   indefinite   indefinite   definite

In addition, there are some special cases of article use.

1. Use no article and a plural noun to refer to people from most countries and cultures. However, *the* + a singular noun is used for some other national and cultural groups.

   <u>Mexicans</u> and <u>Guatemalans</u> live in the region once occupied by <u>the Maya</u> and <u>the Olmec</u>.

2. Use no article with most proper nouns. Exceptions include certain countries (*the United States, the United Kingdom, the Philippines*), rivers (*the Nile, the Yangtze*), oceans (*the Atlantic, the Indian Ocean*), and mountain ranges (*the Alps, the Andes*).

A. Complete the paragraph with *a*, *an*, and *the*. If no article is needed, write X.

(1) _____The_____ indigenous people of (2) _____ Australia are called Aboriginals. (3) _____ tribes were living on (4) _____ Australian continent long before (5) _____ arrival of (6) _____ British colonists in (7) _____ late eighteenth century. (8) _____ researchers estimate that there were 250 Aboriginal languages at that time. Today, just over 100 languages are just spoken by (9) _____ older people, but only 18 languages have (10) _____ speakers of all (11) _____ ages. One of (12) _____ reasons for (13) _____ decline in (14) _____ native cultures was (15) _____ Australian government's policies. In 2008, Prime Minister Kevin Rudd made (16) _____ remarkable decision. He issued (17) _____ apology to (18) _____ Aboriginal people of Australia for all (19) _____ pain and loss that they had suffered. (20) _____ apology has raised awareness about Australia's native history.

B. Correct all the errors with articles in the paragraph.

The s
^ Study of ancient civilizations attempts to answer questions about where the humans came from and how the civilizations rose and fell. Ancient civilizations were usually built near a good source of the water. For an instance, the ancient Babylonians built thriving empire between the Tigris and Euphrates Rivers in Middle East. First record of the Babylon, the capital of Babylonia, dates to about 3800 BCE. Despite rivers, the area did not receive much rain, so early engineers devised the pump to bring water to the gardens.

WRITING SKILL   Introductions and Conclusions

LEARN

A good introduction gives the reader enough background knowledge to understand the rest of the paper, and it states the focus, or thesis, of the paper. It is important for all the sentences in the introduction to be relevant to the paper. Avoid starting with very broad, general statements.

The content of the conclusion depends on the type of writing, but conclusions are often short. In academic writing, the conclusion might do some of the following things:

- discuss the importance of the ideas in the paper

- explain why further research is needed

- make a prediction about future developments or changes

- remind the reader of the focus or thesis

- leave the reader with a final thought

APPLY

A. Look again at the introduction to the synthesis on page 142. Underline the sentence that contains the focus of the paper. Compare your answer with a partner.

B. Look again at the conclusion of the synthesis on page 144. Which functions of a conclusion do you see? Compare your answer with a partner.

explain why further research is needed

_____

_____

_____

_____

Collaborative Writing

A. Some of the sentences below could be used in the introduction or conclusion to an essay about the Ojibwa, a tribe native to the United States and Canada. Work in a small group and decide which sentences you would use in the introduction (*I*), the conclusion (*C*), or not at all (*X*).

1. I / C / X   The future remains uncertain.

2. I / C / X   Poverty rates among the Ojibwa are high and educational achievement is often low.

3. I / C / X   Traveling through the Great Lakes region, it is impossible to ignore the traces of its first people, among whom are the Ojibwa.

4. I / C / X   Today, few Ojibwa speak their native language or follow their traditional customs.

5. I / C / X   Without more interest from young people, support from the authorities, and improved infrastructure, progress may not be sustained.

6. I / C / X   There are many native cultures in the world.

7. I / C / X   *Michigan*—the name of the state and the lake—is an Ojibwa word, denoting "big water."

8. I / C / X   The Ojibwa were once the predominant tribe in the region.

9. I / C / X   Attempts to transmit Ojibwa culture to the next generation are essential to solve social problems and save an important piece of the region's traditions.

10. I / C / X   In conclusion, there are signs that the Ojibwa language and culture are already making a comeback.

11. I / C / X   In my essay, I am going to write about the Ojibwa people.

B. With your group, write the introduction and conclusion paragraphs for an essay about the Ojibwa. You will need to add transitions. You can also add sentences.

C. Share your paragraphs with another group. Discuss these questions.

1. Did you choose the same sentences from activity B for your introduction and conclusion?

2. Did you choose the same order for the sentences? Explain your group's choices.

3. Do your paragraphs have unity and cohesion?

4. Is the focus of the essay clear?

5. What information would you expect to read in the rest of the essay?

Independent Writing

A. You are going to write a synthesis of two articles. First, read the two articles about the Olmec writing system on page 158. Do the writers agree about the answers to these questions? Complete the chart.

Question	Answer(s)	Agree?
1. What is the block and where was it found?	*A piece of stone with inscriptions that may be written characters, found in a pile of debris.* *Bruhns & Kelker: "Cascajal block"*	Yes
2. Did the Olmec produce writing?		
3. Are the inscriptions on the Cascajal block writing?		
4. Are the characters arranged like writing?		
5. Did the Olmec make the inscriptions on the block?		
6. Were the Olmec the dominant culture of the region?		

B. In addition to the answers you wrote in activity A, are there any other important ideas in the two articles that you want to include in a synthesis?

Lawler, 2006	Bruhns & Kelker, 2007

C. Choose how you will organize a synthesis of these two articles. Complete **one** of the outlines.

Introduction: Description of the Cascajal block	
Points of agreement:	
Lawler's argument:	
Bruhns & Kelker's argument:	
Conclusion:	

Introduction: Description of the Cascajal block	
Points of agreement:	
Disagreement 1:	
Disagreement 2:	
Disagreement 3:	
Conclusion:	

D. Choose the correct word or phrase to complete each sentence.

1. (Unlike / While) the Olmec, the Maya lived in the areas that are now Honduras, El Salvador, and Belize.

2. Inomata et al. (similarly / disagree) with Blomster et al. about the date of the fall of San Lorenzo.

3. The Maya built great cities with formal public buildings. (Whereas / Likewise), Olmec cities in their later period had pyramids and other administrative buildings.

4. Tourists visit many ancient Maya sites. The Olmec are less well known, (though / similarly).

VOCABULARY TIP

Here are some words and phrases you can use to show similarities and differences between authors' ideas:

agree (with), also, disagree (with), like, likewise, on the other hand, similarly, though, unlike, whereas, while

E. Write two sentences about agreements between the Lawler (2006) and Bruhns & Kelker (2007) articles, and write two sentences about disagreements between them. Use a different word or phrase from the Vocabulary Tip in each sentence.

1. _____

2. _____

3. _____

4. _____

F. Write a synthesis of the two articles (Lawler, 2006, and Bruhns & Kelker, 2007). Use the ideas in activity A and the organization in activity B. As you write, include phrases from activities C and D. Use target vocabulary from page 141.

REVISE AND EDIT

A. Read your synthesis. Answer the questions below, and make revisions as needed.

1. Check (✓) the information you included in your case analysis.

☐ introduction with background information and a focus

☐ conclusion with a restatement, final thought, or prediction

☐ points of agreement between the articles

☐ citations and references

☐ several points of disagreement between the articles

2. Look at the information you did not include. Would adding that information make your synthesis more interesting?

Grammar for Editing   Countable and Uncountable Nouns

1. With countable nouns, you can use *many, few, a few, fewer,* and *a number of.*

2. With uncountable nouns, you can use *much, little, a little, less,* and *a large/small amount of.*

    much
There is not ~~many~~ information about the Olmec.

3. Singular countable nouns must have an article or other determiner (e.g., *one, any, this, my, your, its*). Uncountable nouns often have no article.

    a
According to ^recent study, writing existed in South America earlier than previously thought.

4. Uncountable nouns have no plural form.

Scientists have found evidences of an ancient civilization in this region.

5. Many uncountable nouns can become countable with a small change in meaning.

Linguistics is the study of *language*. (uncountable: general idea)

The Olmec may have had *a written language*. (countable: specific example)

B. Check the language in your synthesis. Revise and edit as needed.

Language Checklist
☐ I used target words in my synthesis.
☐ I used words and phrases to show similarities and differences.
☐ I used articles correctly.
☐ I used countable and uncountable nouns correctly.

C. Check your synthesis again. Repeat activities A and B.

Self-Assessment Review: Go back to page 141 and reassess your knowledge of the target vocabulary. How has your understanding of the words changed? What words do you feel most comfortable using now?

Resources

What Humans Know that Watson Doesn't

by Trevor Pinch, posted on CNN.com

Note: Watson is the name of an IBM supercomputer. Watson competed against two humans on the American TV quiz show "Jeopardy!" Watson won.

One of my most frustrating experiences is dealing with airlines' automated answer systems. Your flight has just been canceled and every second counts in getting a seat. Yet you are stuck in an automated menu spelling out the name of your destination city.

It is even more frustrating knowing that you will never get to ask the question you really want to ask, as it isn't an option: "If I drive to New York and board my flight to London there rather than Ithaca, where I am now, will you cancel my whole trip?" A human would immediately understand the question and give you an answer. That's why knowledgeable travelers rush to the nearest airport when they experience a cancellation and talk to a human agent.

There is no doubt the IBM supercomputer Watson gave an impressive performance on "Jeopardy!" this week. But I was worried by the computer's biggest mistake. The question was to name a U.S. city whose first airport is named after a World War II hero and its second after a World War II battle. Watson answered Toronto, a city in Canada. Both the humans on the program knew the correct answer: Chicago. Even I knew the answer, and I come from the UK!

Why did I know it? Because I have spent enough time stranded[1] at Chicago's O'Hare Airport to have visited the monument[2] to Butch O'Hare in the terminal. Watson, who has not, came up with the wrong answer. This reveals precisely what Watson lacks—life experience. Watson has never traveled anywhere. Humans travel, so we know all sorts of stuff about travel and airports that a computer doesn't know. It is the informal knowledge and

"Jeopardy!" champions Ken Jennings, left, and Brad Rutter, right, flank a prop representing Watson during a practice round of the "Jeopardy!" quiz show.

life experience that is the hardest for computers to grasp. However, it is often such knowledge that is most crucial to our lives.

Providing unique answers to questions limited to around 25 words is not the same as dealing with real problems of an unhappy passenger in an open system where there may not be a unique answer. Watson beating us on "Jeopardy!" is fun—rather like seeing a tractor beat a human tug-of-war[3] team. Machines have always been better than humans at some tasks. It is no big deal.[4]

The big deal is when technology is overhyped.[5] For example, IBM talks about Watson revolutionizing[6] whole industries. Humans know hype when they see it, just like they know that dealing with airline reservation systems under crisis is about the worst experience possible, especially when the computer insists that your destination is in Canada rather than in the United States. ∎

Trevor Pinch is a professor of science and technology studies at Cornell University in the United States.

---

[1] *stranded:* left in a place with no way of leaving
[2] *monument:* a statue. built to remind people of a famous person
[3] *tug-of-war:* a sports event in which two teams pull at opposite ends of a rope until one team drags the other over a line on the ground
[4] *no big deal:* not very important
[5] *overhype:* to greatly exaggerate something's good qualities in order to get a lot of public attention for it
[6] *revolutionize:* to completely change the way that something is done

Reprint info: "For web posting, reprint, transcript or licensing requests for CNN material, please contact licensing.agent@turner.com"

Claim of Oldest New World Writing Excites Archaeologists

Andrew Lawler, Science (News), September 15, 2006

A stone block uncovered in a Mexican quarry[1] provides dramatic evidence that the ancient Olmec people developed a writing system as early as 900 BCE, according to seven Mesoamerican scholars writing in

5 this week's issue of Science. That makes the block's 62-sign inscription[2] by far the oldest writing discovered in the New World.[3] The discovery also hints at surprising complexity in a culture that may have laid the foundation for the Mayan and Aztec empires.

10 Road builders digging an ancient hill at Cascajal, outside San Lorenzo, found the new block together with pottery fragments. The local official with responsibility for cultural materials stored the objects in his home and alerted anthropologists María del Carmen

15 Rodríguez Martínez and Ponciano Ortiz Ceballos. The block was then examined by the entire team this spring. The authors argue that the block is roughly the same age as the artifacts[4] found with it, which they say date to the latter part of the Olmecs' San Lorenzo phase.[5]

20 The entire find was located fairly close to San Lorenzo. Therefore, Martínez and her colleagues believe that the block was made in San Lorenzo by the Olmec. This makes it the oldest known writing in Mesoamerica and supports the theory that the Olmec were the

25 dominant culture of their time. Co-author Stephen Houston of Brown University goes a step further, saying "We're looking, possibly, at the glimmerings of an early empire."

Most experts agree that the inscription qualifies as

30 writing and therefore is a dramatic find. This is because a few of the signs are repeated, and there are patterns and repeated sequences. "The Cascajal block conforms to all the expectations of writing," the authors say. The writing's influence on later systems is unclear, however.

35 The text appears to run horizontally rather than vertically as in later Mesoamerican scripts. Nor can the writing be linked with a later writing system, Isthmian, which has radically different signs. Nevertheless, the authors conclude that Olmec writing

40 was a widespread system that died out before others appeared in later centuries.

---

[1] *quarry:* a place where large amounts of stone are dug out of the ground
[2] *inscription:* words cut in stone
[3] *New World:* North, Central, and South America
[4] *artifact:* an object made by a person, especially something of historical or cultural interest
[5] *phase:* period of time

DID THE OLMEC KNOW HOW TO WRITE?

Karen O. Bruhns, San Francisco State University
Nancy L. Kelker, Middle Tennessee State University, Science, March 9, 2007

In their research article "Earliest Writing in America," del Carmen Rodríguez Martínez et al. (2007) suggest that the inscribed "Cascajal block" is the first discovery of Olmec writing. Although we

5 agree with the authors that it is possible the Olmec did write, we have strong reservations[1] concerning this particular discovery.

First, being found by unknown people in a pile of debris[2] is not a reliable origin. Furthermore,

10 the block does not fit any known category of Mesoamerican artifact. For instance, it is clearly not a sculpture or jewel. The Olmec did not build in stone; therefore, it cannot be an inscription on a building. Indeed, there are many hundreds of similar blocks

15 known at the Olmec city of La Venta, but not a single one of these has engravings. Therefore, we doubt that the signs on the Cascajal block actually came from San Lorenzo or were inscribed by the Olmec.

As for the characters themselves, other

20 Mesoamerican writing systems are written either vertically or linearly. While del Carmen Rodríguez Martínez et al. claim to see a horizontal pattern in the characters, we feel that they randomly "bunch" on the Cascajal block. This is unlike any writing

25 system known to date. Indeed, many of the so-called written characters replicate decorations found on a wide range of largely unprovenanced (i.e., their authenticity is not proved) small-scale artifacts. None of these drawings in their original context has been

30 identified as a form of writing. Finally, one particular symbol, which we can only describe as the "cootie"[3] character, fits no known category of Mesoamerican drawing. This, together with the location of the discovery, strongly suggests that the block is a

35 practical joke and not a genuine historical artifact. Consequently, it is too early to declare the Olmec the mother culture of Mesoamerica.

---

[1] *reservations:* feeling doubt about something
[2] *debris:* pieces of material that are not wanted and trash that is left somewhere
[3] *cootie:* a children's word for a small bug that lives in a person's hair (a nit or louse)

The Academic Word List

Words targeted in Level 4 are bold

Word	Sublist	Location
abandon	8	L2, U6
abstract	6	L3, U1
academy	5	L2, U8
access	4	L0, U6
accommodate	9	L3, U6
accompany	8	**L4, U6**
accumulate	8	L3, U10
accurate	6	L0, U4
achieve	2	L0, U1
acknowledge	6	L0, U7
acquire	2	L3, U4
adapt	7	L0, U3
adequate	4	L3, U3
adjacent	10	**L4, U3**
adjust	5	**L4, U6**
administrate	2	**L4, U10**
adult	7	L0, U8
advocate	7	**L4, U4**
affect	2	L1, U2
aggregate	6	**L4, U5**
aid	7	L3, U4
albeit	10	**L4, U9**
allocate	6	L3, U1
alter	5	L2, U6
alternative	3	L1, U7
ambiguous	8	**L4, U7**
amend	5	**L4, U1**
analogy	9	**L4, U2**
analyze	1	L1, U9
annual	4	L1, U6
anticipate	9	L2, U5
apparent	4	L2, U5
append	8	**L4, U9**
appreciate	8	L0, U8
approach	1	L1, U2
appropriate	2	L3, U4
approximate	4	L2, U1
arbitrary	8	**L4, U7**
area	1	L0, U6
aspect	2	L2, U3
assemble	10	L3, U6
assess	1	L2, U4
assign	6	L3, U9
assist	2	L0, U4
assume	1	L3, U4
assure	9	L3, U9
attach	6	L0, U7

Word	Sublist	Location
attain	9	L3, U5
attitude	4	L2, U4
attribute	4	L3, U3
author	6	L0, U9
authority	1	L2, U9
automate	8	L2, U5
available	1	L0, U8
aware	5	L1, U3
behalf	9	**L4, U1**
benefit	1	L2, U4
bias	8	**L4, U2**
bond	6	**L4, U9**
brief	6	L2, U4
bulk	9	L3, U1
capable	6	L3, U7
capacity	5	**L4, U2**
category	2	L2, U3
cease	9	L2, U8
challenge	5	L1, U2
channel	7	**L4, U3**
chapter	2	L0, U9
chart	8	L0, U8
chemical	7	L2, U10
circumstance	3	**L4, U3**
cite	6	**L4, U7**
civil	4	L3, U10
clarify	8	L3, U8
classic	7	L3, U9
clause	5	L3, U3
code	4	L0, U7
coherent	9	**L4, U6**
coincide	9	**L4, U4**
collapse	10	L3, U6
colleague	10	L3, U1
commence	9	L2, U9
comment	3	L1, U5
commission	2	**L4, U2**
commit	4	L2, U2
commodity	8	**L4, U10**
communicate	4	L1, U3
community	2	L1, U4
compatible	9	L2, U3
compensate	3	**L4, U8**
compile	10	L3, U2
complement	8	**L4, U9**

Word	Sublist	Location
complex	2	L3, U10
component	3	L3, U3
compound	5	L3, U10
comprehensive	7	L3, U3
comprise	7	L3, U1
compute	2	L1, U7
conceive	10	**L4, U4**
concentrate	4	L1, U2
concept	1	L3, U9
conclude	2	L0, U2
concurrent	9	**L4, U3**
conduct	2	L1, U5
confer	4	**L4, U9**
confine	9	**L4, U4**
confirm	7	L1, U10
conflict	5	L1, U10
conform	8	L3, U8
consent	3	L3, U7
consequent	2	**L4, U7**
considerable	3	L3, U9
consist	1	L1, U1
constant	3	L1, U7
constitute	1	**L4, U1**
constrain	3	**L4, U5**
construct	2	L2, U1
consult	5	L2, U2
consume	2	L2, U6
contact	5	L1, U3
contemporary	8	**L4, U3**
context	1	L2, U4
contract	1 L	L3, U4
contradict	8	L2, U4
contrary	7	L3, U8
contrast	4	L3, U5
contribute	3	L1, U4
controversy	9	L2, U1
convene	3	**L4, U8**
converse	9	L2, U10
convert	7	**L4, U9**
convince	10	L1, U9
cooperate	6	L3, U2
coordinate	3	L2, U5
core	3	**L4, U1**
corporate	3	L1, U7
correspond	3	L3, U2
couple	7	L0, U7
create	1	L2, U7

Oxford 3000™ words

Word	Sublist	Location	Word	Sublist	Location	Word	Sublist	Location
credit	2	L2, U9	emphasis	3	L1, U7	**forthcoming**	**10**	**L4, U9**
criteria	3	L3, U3	**empirical**	**7**	**L4, U5**	found	9	L0, U10
crucial	**8**	**L4, U7**	enable	5	L2, U7	foundation	7	L1, U9
culture	2	L0, U9	encounter	10	L1, U5	**framework**	**3**	**L4, U3**
currency	8	L2, U7	energy	5	L0, U1	function	1	L3, U3
cycle	4	L3, U1	**enforce**	**5**	**L4, U7**	fund	3	L2, U9
			enhance	6	L3, U5	fundamental	5	L1, U8
data	1	L0, U3	enormous	10	L0, U2	furthermore	6	L3, U1
debate	4	L3, U5	**ensure**	**3**	**L4, U6**			
decade	7	L1, U9	**entity**	**5**	**L4, U9**	gender	6	L3, U2
decline	5	L1, U6	environment	1	L1, U6	generate	5	L1, U4
deduce	3	L3, U3	equate	2	L3, U2	generation	5	L2, U8
define	1	L0, U6	equip	7	L2, U3	globe	7	L2, U1
definite	**7**	**L4, U6**	equivalent	5	L1, U10	goal	4	L0, U1
demonstrate	3	L1, U5	**erode**	**9**	**L4, U8**	grade	7	L0, U9
denote	**8**	**L4, U10**	error	4	L0, U4	grant	4	L3, U2
deny	7	L1, U10	establish	1	L2, U2	guarantee	7	L1, U4
depress	10	L0, U10	estate	6	L3, U1	guideline	8	L1, U8
derive	**1**	**L4, U2**	estimate	1	L2, U8			
design	2	L0, U3	ethic	9	L3, U8	hence	4	L3, U1
despite	4	L3, U10	ethnic	4	L3, U10	**hierarchy**	**7**	**L4, U10**
detect	8	L2, U1	evaluate	2	L1, U8	highlight	8	L0, U7
deviate	**8**	**L4, U7**	eventual	8	L3, U5	hypothesis	4	L3, U7
device	9	L0, U7	evident	1	L2, U1			
devote	9	L2, U4	evolve	5	L2, U8	identical	7	L3, U7
differentiate	7	L3, U8	exceed	6	L1, U8	identify	1	L1, U5
dimension	**4**	**L4, U9**	exclude	3	L2, U2	**ideology**	**7**	**L4, U3**
diminish	9	L2, U6	exhibit	8	L2, U10	ignorance	6	L2, U10
discrete	**5**	**L4, U10**	expand	5	L0, U2	illustrate	3	L0, U6
discriminate	**6**	**L4, U1**	expert	6	L2, U2	image	5	L1, U7
displace	8	L3, U5	**explicit**	**6**	**L4, U7**	**immigrate**	**3**	**L4, U8**
display	6	L0, U9	**exploit**	**8**	**L4, U7**	impact	2	L2, U6
dispose	**7**	**L4, U8**	export	1	L3, U9	**implement**	**4**	**L4, U7**
distinct	**2**	**L4, U10**	**expose**	**5**	**L4, U8**	implicate	4	L3, U7
distort	**9**	**L4, U7**	external	5	L2, U3	**implicit**	**8**	**L4, U1**
distribute	1	L1, U6	extract	7	L3, U5	imply	3	L3, U5
diverse	**6**	**L4, U3**				impose	4	L3, U8
document	3	L0, U10	facilitate	5	L3, U6	**incentive**	**6**	**L4, U5**
domain	**6**	**L4, U7**	factor	1	L3, U2	incidence	6	L3, U2
domestic	4	L2, U6	feature	2	L0, U5	**incline**	**10**	**L4, U6**
dominate	**3**	**L4, U8**	**federal**	**6**	**L4, U1**	income	1	L3, U2
draft	5	L0, U10	fee	6	L0, U5	**incorporate**	**6**	**L4, U3**
drama	8	L2, U7	file	7	L0, U10	index	6	L4, U8
duration	9	L2, U5	final	2	L0, U3	indicate	1	L2, U3
dynamic	7	L3, U1	finance	1	L3, U4	individual	1	L0, U4
			finite	**7**	**L4, U9**	**induce**	**8**	**L4, U4**
economy	1	L2, U3	flexible	6	L1, U10	**inevitable**	**8**	**L4, U1**
edit	6	L1, U1	**fluctuate**	**8**	**L4, U6**	**infer**	**7**	**L4, U2**
element	2	L3, U9	focus	2	L0, U1	**infrastructure**	**8**	**L4, U10**
eliminate	7	L1, U7	format	9	L2, U1	**inherent**	**9**	**L4, U5**
emerge	**4**	**L4, U10**	formula	1	L3, U8	**inhibit**	**6**	**L4, U5**

Oxford 3000™ words

Word	Sublist	Location
✎ initial	3	L0, U4
initiate	6	L3, U2
✎ **injure**	**2**	**L4, U6**
innovate	7	L3, U3
input	6	L2, U2
insert	7	L2, U7
insight	9	L3, U7
inspect	**8**	**L4, U7**
✎ instance	3	L3, U4
✎ institute	2	L1, U8
instruct	6	L1, U10
integral	**9**	**L4, U5**
integrate	**4**	**L4, U7**
integrity	10	L2, U8
✎ intelligence	6	L0, U8
✎ intense	8	L3, U7
interact	3	L2, U1
intermediate	9	L2, U7
✎ internal	4	L1, U2
interpret	**1**	**L4, U2**
✎ interval	6	L3, U7
intervene	7	L3, U4
intrinsic	**10**	**L4, U5**
✎ invest	2	L3, U9
✎ investigate	4	L2, U9
invoke	**10**	**L4, U9**
✎ involve	1	L3, U10
isolate	7	L3, U4
✎ issue	1	L0, U6
✎ item	2	L0, U5
✎ job	4	L0, U3
journal	2	L1, U9
✎ justify	3	L3, U2
✎ label	4	L0, U5
✎ labor	1	L2, U4
✎ **layer**	**3**	**L4, U10**
✎ lecture	6	L0, U8
✎ legal	1	L1, U3
legislate	**1**	**L4, U1**
levy	**10**	**L4, U4**
✎ **liberal**	**5**	**L4, U3**
✎ license	5	L3, U6
likewise	10	L3, U10
✎ link	3	L0, U5
✎ locate	3	L1, U1
✎ logic	5	L3, U1
✎ maintain	2	L1, U4
✎ major	1	L0, U2

Word	Sublist	Location
manipulate	**8**	**L4, U2**
manual	9	L3, U3
margin	5	L2, U4
mature	9	L2, U8
maximize	3	L1, U7
mechanism	4	L3, U3
✎ media	7	L0, U9
mediate	9	L3, U4
✎ medical	5	L1, U2
✎ medium	9	L1, U10
✎ mental	5	L2, U10
✎ method	1	L1, U3
migrate	**6**	**L4, U10**
✎ military	9	L2, U9
minimal	9	L1, U8
minimize	8	L3, U9
✎ minimum	6	L1, U8
✎ **ministry**	**6**	**L4, U1**
✎ minor	3	L0, U8
mode	7	L3, U2
modify	5	L1, U10
✎ monitor	5	L3, U7
motive	6	L2, U4
mutual	9	L2, U10
negate	**3**	**L4, U8**
✎ network	5	L2, U5
neutral	6	L2, U9
✎ nevertheless	6	L3, U10
nonetheless	**10**	**L4, U6**
norm	**9**	**L4, U5**
✎ normal	2	L0, U3
✎ **notion**	**5**	**L4, U2**
notwithstanding	**10**	**L4, U2**
✎ nuclear	8	L3, U10
✎ objective	5	L0, U4
✎ obtain	2	L3, U1
✎ obvious	4	L1, U5
✎ **occupy**	**4**	**L4, U6**
✎ occur	1	L2, U1
✎ odd	10	L1, U1
offset	8	L3, U2
ongoing	10	L2, U5
✎ option	4	L1, U9
orient	**5**	**L4, U7**
outcome	3	L2, U4
✎ output	4	L2, U3
✎ overall	4	L2, U3
overlap	9	L2, U9
✎ overseas	6	L3, U10

Word	Sublist	Location
✎ **panel**	**10**	**L4, U1**
paradigm	**7**	**L4, U9**
paragraph	8	L1, U1
✎ **parallel**	**4**	**L4, U10**
parameter	4	L3, U8
✎ participate	2	L1, U1
✎ partner	3	L0, U5
passive	9	L3, U8
perceive	**2**	**L4, U6**
✎ percent	1	L1, U7
✎ period	1	L3, U4
persist	10	L3, U7
✎ perspective	5	L2, U3
✎ phase	4	L2, U1
phenomenon	**7**	**L4, U5**
✎ philosophy	3	L3, U9
✎ physical	3	L0, U1
✎ plus	8	L0, U6
✎ policy	1	L2, U8
portion	9	L2, U6
✎ **pose**	**10**	**L4, U2**
✎ positive	2	L0, U1
✎ potential	2	L2, U5
practitioner	**8**	**L4, U4**
precede	6	L3, U8
✎ precise	5	L3, U9
✎ predict	4	L0, U3
predominant	**8**	**L4, U10**
preliminary	9	L2, U5
presume	**6**	**L4, U6**
✎ previous	2	L0, U5
✎ primary	2	L1, U4
prime	**5**	**L4, U6**
✎ principal	4	L2, U7
✎ principle	1	L3, U8
✎ prior	4	L2, U9
✎ priority	7	L2, U5
✎ proceed	1	L2, U7
✎ process	1	L1, U5
✎ professional	4	L1, U8
prohibit	7	L3, U5
✎ project	4	L1, U1
promote	**4**	**L4, U4**
✎ proportion	3	L2, U6
✎ **prospect**	**8**	**L4, U2**
protocol	**9**	**L4, U8**
psychology	5	L2, U6
✎ publication	7	L3, U7
✎ publish	3	L0, U10
✎ purchase	2	L0, U5
✎ **pursue**	**5**	**L4, U1**

✎ Oxford 3000™ words

Word	Sublist	Location	Word	Sublist	Location	Word	Sublist	Location
qualitative	9	**L4, U5**	series	4	L0, U2	**thereby**	7	**L4, U6**
quote	7	L1, U9	**sex**	3	**L4, U5**	thesis	7	L3, U7
radical	8	**L4, U2**	shift	3	L2, U7	topic	7	L0, U7
random	8	L2, U10	significant	1	L3, U7	**trace**	6	**L4, U10**
range	2	L2, U3	similar	1	L1, U6	tradition	2	L0, U9
ratio	5	L3, U6	simulate	7	L3, U3	transfer	2	L1, U6
rational	6	L3, U8	site	2	L1, U1	transform	6	L3, U1
react	3	L1, U5	so-called	10	L2, U1	transit	5	L2, U2
recover	6	L2, U5	**sole**	7	**L4, U4**	**transmit**	7	**L4, U10**
refine	9	L3, U1	somewhat	7	L3, U5	transport	6	L1, U8
regime	4	L3, U10	source	1	L1, U6	trend	5	L1, U3
region	2	L3, U10	specific	1	L1, U3	**trigger**	9	**L4, U4**
register	3	L3, U9	specify	3	L1, U9			
regulate	2	L3, U3	**sphere**	9	**L4, U2**	ultimate	7	L3, U9
reinforce	8	L3, U6	stable	5	L3, U6	**undergo**	10	**L4, U4**
reject	5	L1, U10	statistic	4	L2, U10	**underlie**	6	**L4, U5**
relax	9	L0, U4	status	4	L0, U9	**undertake**	4	**L4, U3**
release	7	L1, U6	straightforward	10	L3, U3	uniform	7	L2, U10
relevant	2	L3, U2	strategy	2	L2, U2	unify	9	L2, U9
reluctance	10	L2, U8	stress	4	L0, U1	unique	7	L2, U7
rely	3	L2, U6	structure	1	L2, U7	utilize	6	L3, U6
remove	3	L0, U8	style	5	L2, U2			
require	1	L0, U3	submit	7	L1, U10	valid	3	L3, U8
research	1	L0, U2	**subordinate**	9	**L4, U9**	vary	1	L1, U2
reside	2	**L4, U4**	subsequent	4	L3, U5	vehicle	7	L2, U2
resolve	4	L2, U4	**subsidy**	6	**L4, U3**	version	5	L1, U9
resource	2	L0, U4	substitute	5	L2, U6	**via**	7	**L4, U3**
respond	1	L1, U4	successor	7	L3, U8	violate	9	L3, U6
restore	8	L2, U5	**sufficient**	3	**L4, U1**	virtual	8	L3, U5
restrain	9	L3, U6	sum	4	L3, U5	visible	7	L0, U2
restrict	2	L2, U6	summary	4	L1, U3	vision	9	L2, U2
retain	4	**L4, U8**	supplement	9	L2, U10	visual	8	L2, U7
reveal	6	L2, U10	survey	2	L2, U9	volume	3	L1, U7
revenue	5	L3, U9	survive	7	L2, U8	voluntary	7	L3, U4
reverse	7	L3, U4	**suspend**	9	**L4, U1**			
revise	8	L1, U8	sustain	5	L3, U6	**welfare**	5	**L4, U4**
revolution	9	**L4, U3**	symbol	5	L0, U10	**whereas**	5	**L4, U5**
rigid	9	L2, U8				**whereby**	10	**L4, U8**
role	1	L0, U7	tape	6	L3, U5	widespread	7	L3, U4
route	9	L3, U10	target	5	L2, U2			
			task	3	L0, U6			
scenario	9	L2, U8	team	9	L0, U1			
schedule	7	L1, U2	technical	3	L3, U6			
scheme	3	**L4, U8**	technique	3	L3, U6			
scope	6	L2, U10	technology	3	L2, U3			
section	1	L0, U2	temporary	9	L0, U6			
sector	1	**L4, U9**	tense	7	L2, U1			
secure	2	L1, U4	**terminate**	7	**L4, U8**			
seek	2	L2, U9	text	2	L0, U10			
select	2	L1, U6	theme	7	L1, U9			
sequence	3	L1, U6	theory	1	L3, U7			

Oxford 3000™ words